About the author

Nikki van der Gaag is an independent writer
and consultant based in the UK. She has been
involved in feminism and development for more
than 20 years and has held senior editorial and
communications posts in the non-profit sector,
including at Oxfam, the *New Internationalist* and
the Panos Institute. She specializes in writing
about gender, in particular girls' issues, and
men and gender equality. She is the principal
author of six of the eight *State of the World's
Girls* reports and has written nine other books,
including *The No-nonsense Guide to Women's
Rights*.

FEMINISM AND MEN

Nikki van der Gaag

Zed Books
LONDON

Fernwood Publishing
HALIFAX | WINNIPEG

Feminism and Men was first published in 2014 by Zed Books Ltd, 7 Cynthia Street, London N1 9JF, UK.

www.zedbooks.co.uk

Published in Canada by Fernwood Publishing, 32 Oceanvista Lane, Black Point, Nova Scotia, B0J 1B0 and 748 Broadway Avenue, Winnipeg, Manitoba, R3G 0X3.

www.fernwoodpublishing.ca

Set in Monotype Plantin and FFKievit by Ewan Smith, London
Index: ed.emery@thefreeuniversity.net
Cover design: www.kikamiller.com

Fernwood Publishing Company Limited gratefully acknowledges the financial support of the Government of Canada through the Canada Book Fund and the Canada Council for the Arts, the Nova Scotia Department of Communities, Culture and Heritage, the Manitoba Department of Culture, Heritage and Tourism under the Manitoba Book Publishers Marketing Assistance Program and the Province of Manitoba, through the Book Publishing Tax Credit, for our publishing program.

A catalogue record for this book is available from the British Library
Library of Congress Cataloging in Publication Data available
Cataloguing data available from Library and Archives Canada

ISBN 978-1-78032-912-3 hb (Zed Books)
ISBN 978-1-78032-911-6 pb (Zed Books)
ISBN 978-1-55266-694-4 pb (Fernwood Publishing)

Printed and bound in Great Britain by
TJ International Ltd, Padstow, Cornwall

CONTENTS

FIGURES

ACKNOWLEDGEMENTS

This book has been a long time in the making, and is the product of many discussions with many men and women and girls and boys on different continents – thanks to all of you.

In particular I would like to thank Ruth Pearson for her support throughout, Gary Barker and Michael Kaufman for commenting on the draft and contributing to so many of the ideas behind it, Tina Wallace for discussions over many years on gender equality, and Sharon Goulds for working with me on the ideas for Plan's *Because I Am a Girl* report on boys and gender equality.

Thanks too to Kat Banyard for discussions on young women and feminism, and to Sandy Ruxton, Kirrily Pells, Emma Wilson and Caroline Knowles; to Rachel Ploem for sharing ideas on balancing feminism and work on masculinities and to Marisa Viana da Silva, Oswaldo Montoya Telleria and Marc Peters, and all those among the 'unlikely encounter of unusual suspects' at the 'Undressing Patriarchy' conference organized by the Institute of Development Studies. And of course to the many hundreds of people who answered my online survey for this book – your time and effort were much appreciated.

Thanks to Sarah Lewis for her meticulous research, and to the editors at Zed Books, including Tamsine O'Riordan and Jakob Horstmann, who were so enthusiastic about the idea, and to Kim Walker for the process of putting the whole thing together with Ewan Smith, copyeditor Ian Paten and proofreader Chris Parker. To my mother, Mary, for her support, and my late father, Gerth, who would not necessarily have agreed with all the ideas but would have been proud of me for writing this book. And finally to Margaret Mowles, and to my partner Chris for his love, patience and careful comments, and my grown-up children Rosa and George, for listening to my rants for so many years.

1 | INTRODUCTION

Time to change: men and feminism

'Women are strong, bold, and brave, but men and boys
also have a big role to play in ending gender inequality.
... It's time to influence change in society.' (Phumzile
Mlambo-Ngcuka, United Nations under-secretary-general,
March 2014)[1]

Phumzile Mlambo-Ngcuka's open letter to men asking them to
support women's struggle for gender equality comes at just the
right time.

For the last few decades, there have been fundamental
changes to the way that many women all over the world live
their lives. They have moved into paid work in unprecedented
numbers. They have challenged sexism and discrimination and
gender inequality and violence. In many countries, girls are not
only going to school but doing as well as or better than boys and
young men. A raft of new laws have been enacted at international
and national level to protect women's rights.

At the same time, social and economic inequalities have been
growing, and together with increasing religious and cultural conservatism threaten to undermine many of the gains women have
made. A recent United Nations report[2] notes that the progress
made in the past twenty years towards reducing global poverty is
at risk of being reversed because of a failure to combat widening
inequality and strengthen women's rights.

But some things have not changed. Men still hold the majority of positions of power. Men's violence against women, which cuts across race, class and geography, shows no sign of decreasing. And women and girls in many countries continue to be seen as second-class citizens, especially if they are poor, or come from a black or minority ethnic group.

However, one of the consequences of the changes in women's lives is that the traditional model of being a man – the strong leader and main provider of the household – is slowly beginning to be questioned, not just by the 'bold and brave' women invoked by Phumzile Mlambo-Ngcuka, but by some men as well. Men like Anthony, or Pascal, both of whom we meet later in this book. Anthony had to learn how to move beyond the belief that his wife Janine should do as she was told. And Pascal found that he was becoming a violent man just like his father and didn't know what to do about it.

This growing group of men in many parts of the world don't want to react as they see some other men do, with violence bred of frustration. They experience power over women, but they find that does not necessarily make them happy.

And while, in many countries, girls and women, despite many setbacks, continue to have an increasing number of choices about who they can be and how they can express themselves, men and boys generally have more restrictive models of what it means to be a man. This is partly because, as Todd Minerson, from the White Ribbon campaign[3] of men opposed to violence against women, notes: 'When you're from the dominant group you don't have that history of struggle and analysis that comes from the non-dominant group's perspective. It's not natural, or it's not something taught. It's not something that's shared with us by our fathers.'[4]

As we will see later in this book, there are alternatives. Men too can change. When shown other ways of thinking and behaving, Anthony and Pascal were able to find a way of being that freed them up to be who they wanted to be – and which benefited the women in their lives as well.

There is also growing interest in the ways in which men can support gender equality, for example the recent campaign 'He for She' by UN Women, which asks men to come forward to say that they support women's rights.[5]

But these changes are not straightforward. There are major differences between men like these who support feminism and gender equality, and those who have reacted by becoming part of a 'men's rights' movement. These men feel that their own needs and voices are being ignored in the debates around gender equality – and that feminism is to blame. And they want to make those voices heard, and they are generally raging against women.

There is a resurgence of feminism in many parts of the world. But there are tensions among feminists, who feel that the movement of men for gender equality is taking away precious space and scarce resources from women's rights activism.

This book explores these sometimes contradictory trends and ideas. It challenges women and men who share the same vision of gender equality to support the widening of the feminist revolution to include men more broadly, without losing the focus on women that remains at its heart.

Feminism and men for gender equality: together or apart?

Marisa Viana da Silva and Oswaldo Montoya Telleria both see themselves as part of this revolution. Marisa is part of the new young feminist wave that is sweeping the world, and Oswaldo one of the growing number of men who base themselves firmly in a feminist tradition in fighting for gender equality.

Marisa, from Brazil, can't pinpoint exactly when she became a feminist. But she is clear that the seeds were sown at a young age: 'I was aware that there were differences between men and women in my family – for example, my brothers had more freedom than my sisters and me. They were allowed to travel to villages near by to play football, but we were not. And my mum never learned to read or write so my dad was the one who owned our properties and took care of the finances.'

Marisa comes from a remote area of the Amazon. She didn't go to school until she was eleven because there was no school where she lived. Then she moved to the city with her brother so that they could both be educated. They stayed with their married sister. Marisa worked hard and caught up with her peers within a year, while her brother struggled. But this didn't make any difference to her life outside school:

> It didn't matter how smart I was, I still wasn't allowed to play outside while my brother was – even though I would finish my homework and chores first. Then when we were fourteen and fifteen my sister went to the USA for three months and my brother became the one in charge. Following the rules that I was not allowed to be out, he used to lock me in the house after six while he went out. My sister said it was to keep me safe.
>
> I think that this awareness of the difference between what boys and girls were allowed to do, and the sense of injustice emerging from that, was one of the reasons why today I call myself a feminist.[6]

Marisa now works in New York for the Young Feminist Activist programme of the Association of Women's Rights in Development.[7]

Oswaldo Montoya Telleria, from Nicaragua, says his involvement in feminism came from working together with women for social change during the revolution:

> The push for involving men came from feminist organizations. Our feminist colleagues would challenge us all the time. It was not naive support for men's involvement, we had strong political discussions and debates. Some women were more reluctant [to involve men in feminist organizing]; others were more open and supportive. But no one is the owner of truth.
>
> The work that we were doing [on gender equality] proved to women that there was a need [for men to be involved]. For example, as men, we were able to reach out to sectors of society that women could not so easily – the police, the military. Because of the long history of sexism in our country, some men started talking about gender equality and others started listening. We provided an alternative for men, proof that we were supporting women but that it was also in our own interest to change. You can continue being a man and embrace this feminist vision. And other men will see the change in you.[8]

Oswaldo is now the coordinator of the MenEngage network, a global alliance of NGOs and UN agencies that seeks to engage boys and men to achieve gender equality.[9]

Both Oswaldo and Marisa support women's rights as part of an awareness of wider social injustices, but they come to it from their own personal experience – Marisa as the indigenous girl from a rural area who was treated differently from her brothers, and Oswaldo from his history in the struggle for justice and as a man in a feminist organization.

At present, feminism and the work of men for gender equality seem to be moving along separate tracks. This book will argue that they need to stop seeing themselves as parallel, or even competing, trends, and come together in order to effect real change.

And for this to happen, the key question to ask is: is there a place for men in the feminist revolution? And do men want to be part of it?

Why write this book?

My son George, aged about eight, was standing in our local supermarket when he suddenly asked me: 'Mum, why are you obsessed with women's rights?' He had a strong role model in his father but he was also exploring what it meant to be male – and I realized that my writing and activism and feminism were mainly about women.

I had already been working on, and writing about, women's rights for many years at that point. My feminism grew out of social activism as a young woman, and the realization in my own life that girls and boys were still treated, and expected to behave, differently. I wanted my daughter Rosa to have as many opportunities in life as my son.

But now George was exploring his place in this debate. He set me thinking about whether I might need a new perspective, one that was more inclusive of men and boys, not just on the periphery but as central to what gender equality was about. Having a son and a daughter gave me new perspectives on my own feminism, and what gender equality really meant.

His question remained with me in the following fifteen years as I undertook research projects with women and girls, and came across men and men's groups who were struggling with their role in debates on gender equality.

I began to realize that other people were thinking about how to involve men in feminism. I started reading books on men and masculinities. I encountered boys and men in many countries who were answering my son's unspoken question by working, slowly and painfully, on what it meant to be a man, learning what Australian pioneer R. W. Connell explained: that there was not one kind of 'masculinity', as so many people seemed to assume, but many forms of masculinities, which change through time and according to class, age, geography, race, sexual orientation and other factors.[10]

I met hundreds of women and girls too, who were still suffering at the hands of men and who were a long way from equality and who were often angry. Some felt threatened by men entering what they saw as a woman-only struggle. They wanted to protect the spaces and resources that had been won with such hard toil over many years. And many of my feminist friends were also suspicious of the motives of men who said they wanted to be involved in women's rights. But there were others who believed that it was vital for men to be engaged in feminism in order for it to succeed.

Then there were the men who brusquely rejected any idea that there was more than one way of being a man. They clung firmly to traditional ideas of what it means to be a man, which we will explore further in the next chapter of this book.

Finally, there were many other men, perhaps even the majority, who continue to live within the power that patriarchy creates between them because of class, race and other factors, but whose experiences of that power are extremely contradictory. They may never even realize that these experiences of unequal power are about gender and about masculinities.

What this book brings to the debates

There have been many books written about feminism, some about masculinities, but only a few that bring feminism and men together. This book is not a history of the involvement of men in feminist or pro-feminist organizing, but rather a view from a particular moment in time that takes a global perspective, bringing together the feminist discourse with the movement of men for gender equality in a worldwide context.

Men's role in the women's movement and how they have been affected by it, both negatively and positively, was described in 1990 by British author Lynne Segal in *Slow Motion: Changing Masculinities, Changing Men* and by American journalist Susan Faludi in *Stiffed: The Betrayal of the Modern Man* in 1999. In 2003, bell hooks wrote *The Will to Change: Men, Masculinities and Love*. In 2012 Hanna Roisin wrote *The End of Men and the Rise of Women*.

There are also examinations and analyses of masculinities and how they are or are not changing, with R. W. Connell the pioneer, but also the *International Encyclopedia of Men and Masculinities* edited by Michael Flood, Judith Kegan Gardiner, Bob Pease and Keith Pringle.

There are fewer books that examine the issue from a non-Western perspective, the edited volume by Sandy Ruxton, *Gender Equality and Men: Learning from Practice*, being one, and *Men and Development: Politicizing Masculinities*, edited by Andrea Cornwall, Jerker Edström and Alan Grieg, another.

There are only a handful that look directly at men's relationship to feminism, all from a Northern perspective. The earliest perhaps is Michael Kimmel and Thomas Mosmiller's 1992 *Against the Tide: Pro-Feminist Men in the United States: 1776–1990, a Documentary History*. In 2002, Amanda Goldrick-Jones wrote *Men Who Believe in Feminism*, a history of anti-sexist men's groups in

North America, Britain and Australia between the 1970s and the 1990s. Tom Digby's 1998 edited volume of essays both personal and academic, *Men Doing Feminism*, is perhaps the most comprehensive, while Shira Tarrant's 2009 *Men and Feminism* gives an overview of men's historical engagement with the feminist movement in the USA. Finally, Michael Kaufman and Michael Kimmel's *The Guy's Guide to Feminism* is a more light hearted 'how to' for men interested in feminism.

Touching a nerve: the process of writing

I wanted to use the books I had read, the increasingly active online presence of arguments on all sides of the debate, and the evidence I had gathered from meeting women and men in many countries over the years I had been working on women's rights, to write a book that would have a wide appeal and would enable readers to think more deeply about men and feminism and the relationship between the two.

In addition, in 2013, I set up an online survey as part of my research. This further convinced me I was on to something. I had hoped for up to a hundred responses. In a few short weeks, I received more than 450 from women and men in many parts of the world. Most were thoughtful. Many were impassioned. This was a topic that clearly touched a nerve. And it also reflected the wide range of attitudes towards feminism. Some disputed the premise of linking men and feminism: 'Making men the centre of a movement. This is what patriarchy is about.' Others were positively in favour: 'I think that gender equality should involve men absolutely. Men and women should not be pitted against one another.'

I had deliberately targeted activist networks, so responses were self-selecting and mainly from people already interested in the topic. I wanted to hear from women and men, from different parts of the world, and from younger and older feminists. The survey was distributed via the campaigning organization UK Feminista,[11] in order to gain access to what younger feminists thought, and via the Gender and Development Network in the UK, the Association of Women's Rights in Development (AWID) and the Men Engage Network. The sample did not aim to be scientifically robust; I was interested in what women and men trying to work differently thought about feminism and gender equality.

Most responses were from women, but 71 (16 per cent) were from men, showing just how much gender and feminism are still seen as a woman's domain. Although the majority were from the European Union, there were responses from every continent, although clearly this was biased in favour of English speakers and those with access to a computer.

It was clear from the comments that respondents varied from those who had been involved in women's rights for a long time and those who were new to feminism. The results will be further elaborated during the course of this book, but two major themes emerged in relation to feminism and men.

First – perhaps reflecting the fact that almost 25 per cent of respondents were under twenty-five – almost 90 per cent of respondents agreed that women benefited from men being involved in gender equality work. This was true of both men and women. Comments included: 'Gender equality cannot be achieved without men. Men need to be at the forefront challenging other men.' Or 'I believe that true equality can only be achieved when people of all ages, ability, gender, race and sexuality work together towards equality.'

A few respondents expressed reservations, for example:

• 'To some extent it depends on which men and why they're

involved – are their motives to genuinely promote gender equality or to promote "men's rights"';

- 'I think however genuine the intent ... the integrity of men will always be looked upon suspiciously by women (a sort of reverse sexism) and be presumed to be an extension to the patriarchy';
- 'Depends on the man, depends on the involvement! I'm not sure some MRAs [men's rights activists] (e.g. in UK Fathers for Justice) are beneficial to gender equality, whereas the White Ribbon Campaign, or Walk a Mile in Her Shoes, is';
- 'The men can understand that it is important to respect women's rights and some progress happens in that way. But when access to certain rights is in conflict with their own rights, there will be a lot of resistance from men'.

Secondly, more than 80 per cent said they believed that men could be feminists, although some qualified this as 'pro-feminist' and a few had reservations:

- 'I think it's unhelpful to use the title [feminist] for men – it is too useful as a group identity for women – men can be supportive of feminist values but do not need to be encompassed in the term. It is politically valuable for women to be able to identify with the multiple feminisms as women';
- 'Only women can be feminists. Men can support feminists and feminist principles';
- 'Can men be feminist? Of course, like as white people can support an end to racism. Patriarchy is a byword for society, we are ALL a part of it. We ALL need to do our bit to see that we bring the world towards equality and enlightenment.'

I was surprised by how positive the majority of respondents were to the idea of men being involved in feminism; though I had no baseline, I expect that this would not have been the case perhaps even a decade ago. And this gave me hope that I was on the right track with the questions I was asking for this book.

The structure of this book

This book has begun with an introduction to the subject of men and feminism. It has explained why I began to be interested in the topic after fifteen years of writing about women's rights; realizing that gender equality will never be achieved without the participation of men as well as women in the struggle for women's rights.

The second chapter moves on to examine men's – and women's – relationship with feminism. Beginning with the journey of one man from violence to advocating for women's rights, it looks at the sometimes extreme reactions by both women and men to the word and the idea of feminism.

Moving on, it shows how men's relationship with feminism is directly bound up with men and women's relationship with LGBTI (lesbian, gay, bisexual, transgender and intersex) issues and examines feminism's uneasy relationship with transgender rights. It asks the crucial question: can men be feminists? How can men work with women to uphold women's rights, and challenge patriarchy and restrictive notions of masculinity? And it looks at men's contradictory experiences of power.

Chapter 3 takes a social view of gender relations and looks at how attitudes towards being a woman or a man are shaped from birth. It explains the negative consequences for girls, for example low self-esteem, or anorexia, and fewer choices in life than their brothers, or, in other countries, a lack of options that mean they have to leave school and marry while they are still children. It shows how conforming to ideas of what it is to be a 'real man' can stifle boys' emotions and lead to homophobia, and how this plays out in different cultures, reinforced by consumerism and the neoliberal agenda. It looks at the influence of consumerism and of pornography on relations between women and men and what this does to our own self-image as well as our relationships with each other. It examines the rise in religious conservatism and its impact on women's rights and how women and men from within their own faith are fighting back against this. Finally, it reveals the differences between generations – and shows what can happen when such attitudes are challenged.

Chapter 4 shows the improvements that have been made in girls' and women's health and education in the past decade. What progress still needs to be made? It argues too that while there needs to be a continuing focus on education for girls and women's health, this has sometimes led to a neglect of boys' education and men's health. Once again, there is no integrated approach that would ensure that all genders – women, men and transgender – are catered for. This chapter lays out the ever-shifting challenges that remain, and addresses the possible consequences if these are not addressed.

Chapter 5 examines the world of employment, and the fact that, on the one hand, there are more women in paid employment than ever before, while on the other, they are still mainly in part-time, badly paid jobs rather than in positions of power and influence, or in the informal sector with no protection at all. This chapter shines a light on this important contradiction, especially in the light of the global economic crisis, where cuts in welfare have hit women hardest and lack of services and support to women in many countries has increased their domestic load greatly. It shows that the economic perspective is hugely different, not just according to which country you live in, but in relation to class, race and poverty. It looks at the importance of the role of provider to men of all backgrounds and in most countries, how this is changing – and what effect this is having on men as well as women. It asks: what can be done to enable men to do more parenting when laws and policies at work are becoming more rather than less flexible?

Chapter 6 is about the changing face of fatherhood around the globe. Four out of five men will become fathers at some point in their lives. But many have no involvement with their children. The chapter outlines what is preventing men being active fathers, and the catalysts for change. It looks at reasons why the fathers' rights movement is so anti-feminist. And it asks: could the increasing number of fathers who are taking an active part in looking after their children constitute a fatherhood revolution? And if men did 50 per cent of the childcare and domestic work, what would this mean for women's ability to participate at work?

Chapter 7 looks directly at men's continuing violence against women. It examines the cultural and social norms that support and promote male violence. It analyses the reasons why some men are violent – and why many are not. It talks about male violence against men and why some feminists find the issue of male rape so difficult. It highlights men's campaigns against violence and asks: what works?

Because unless men like Oswaldo and Todd and others who are interviewed in this book – and other men in the institutions which by and large they still run – are involved alongside women in advocating for the rights of their wives, girlfriends, daughters, sisters, nieces and granddaughters, all the struggles and sacrifices that women have made may be in vain.

2 | BEYOND THE BINARIES: FEMINISM AND MEN

Clearing the way: a man's journey towards feminism

'Feminists offered an important critique about a male-dominated society that routinely, and globally, treated women like second-class citizens. They spoke the truth, and even though I was a man, their truth spoke to me,' said Byron Hurt, African-American documentary film-maker and anti-sexist activist.

> Through feminism, I developed a language that helped me better articulate things that I had experienced growing up as a male. Feminist writings about patriarchy, racism, capitalism and structural sexism resonated with me because I had witnessed firsthand the kind of male dominance they challenged. I saw it as a child in my home and perpetuated it as an adult. Their analysis of male culture and male behavior helped me put my father's patriarchy into a much larger social context, and also helped me understand myself better.
>
> I decided that I loved feminists and embraced feminism. Not only does feminism give woman a voice, but it also clears the way for men to free themselves from the stranglehold of traditional masculinity. When we hurt the women in our lives, we hurt ourselves, and we hurt our community, too.[1]

Hurt is able to articulate very clearly what he felt feminism had to offer him. But many others, both men and women, are much more conflicted. This chapter deals directly with some of the still-emerging themes of contemporary feminist debates about men and feminism. It looks at what feminism means to both men and women, and examines the men's rights movement, which is often implicitly or explicitly anti-women. It shows how men's relationship with feminism is directly bound up with men and women's relationship with LGBTI (lesbian, gay, bisexual, transgender and intersex) issues. It examines twenty-first-century feminism's uneasy relationship with transgender rights. And it hears from a number of men who call themselves feminists about why they think this is so important.

What kind of feminist are you?

For its November 2013 issue, *Elle* magazine commissioned three advertising agencies to undertake what they called a 're-branding' of feminism. One agency produced a flow chart called 'Are You a Feminist?' Another created an ad about equal pay. The third came up with an ad about stereotypes of women.[2] *Elle*'s rationale for the venture was that only one in seven women in the UK call themselves feminists. And only the first of the three agencies' 'rebranding' offered the possibility that men could also be involved.

In fact, the one-in-seven figure came from a survey by Net-mums, an online network for new mothers, so it is not representative of the wider population. For this constituency, it was perhaps not surprising that the top concern (69 per cent) was to 'reinstate the value of motherhood'. On the other hand, 41 per cent felt UK society was 'still a man's world' and 36 per cent said 'their daughters could not imagine a time when men and women were not regarded as equal'.[3]

In locating my own feminism, while I consider myself broadly socially progressive, internationalist, critical of capitalism and particularly neoliberalism, I don't find labels particularly helpful.

I have always liked the simple definition given by Rebecca West, writer and activist, in 1913: 'I myself have never been able to find out precisely what feminism is; I only know that people call me a feminist whenever I express sentiments that differentiate me from a doormat.'

The other insight that holds true for me is 'the personal is political'. It dates back to the 1970s, and remains with me as I write this book. Partly because it continues to be important that we try to practise in our own lives what we 'preach' to others. But also because the two are so intertwined, and yet we often strive to separate them. This perspective was lost some time in the 1990s, when the overall analysis was that we were in a 'post-feminist' era, where many of the rights that earlier feminists were claiming had been achieved.

The main movements of feminists include radical feminists, who prioritize women-only spaces, liberal feminists, and Marxist or socialist feminists, who link their feminism clearly to a critique of capitalism and an analysis of exploitation. Feminists have also formed alliances based on their unique perspectives and experiences of religion, class or race, so there are black feminists, Muslim feminists and lesbian feminist groups and organizations.

Feminism has to be rooted in social, political and cultural realities. Feminist publisher Urvashi Butalia, from India, points out: 'I believe that feminist movements everywhere in the world are born of the particular political and economic realities of the places where they exist. In that sense, each movement has different issues and concerns.' However, she continues: 'Despite cultural and economic differences, there are issues that women share worldwide that have been the concern of feminists.'[4]

Feminism has its own divisions, between young and older, black and white heterosexuals and LGBTI and between countries in the North and those in the South, sometimes called the 'Majority World'. For example, some Southern activists see feminism as a Northern cultural concept, while white middle-class feminists have often failed to understand the racism and oppression faced by black and minority ethnic women.

Bell hooks, long-time feminist activist, academic and writer, and now Distinguished Professor in Residence in Appalachian Studies at Berea College in the USA, offered a broad definition of feminism which does not pit women against men: 'Simply put, feminism is a movement to end sexism, sexist exploitation, and oppression.'[5] She sees this struggle as clearly allied to changing patriarchal structures:

> No matter their standpoint, anyone who advocates feminist politics needs to understand the work does not end with the fight for equality of opportunity within the existing patriarchal structure. We must understand that challenging and dismantling patriarchy is at the core of contemporary feminist struggle – this is essential and necessary if women and men are to be truly liberated from outmoded sexist thinking and actions.[6]

American feminist blogger Jessica Hoffman wrote in her 'Letter to white feminists' that: 'Privilege is a kind of poison – insidious, it obscures, misleads, confuses – and this is part of how power is maintained, as well-meaning privileged people miss the mark, can't clearly see what's going on and how we're implicated, are able to comfortably see ourselves as not responsible.'[7]

Most women are not affected by sexism alone. As one blog on black feminism noted, if it fails to recognize these different oppressions, feminism fails 'to capture and reflect the extreme differences in how women live their lives', which inhibit 'the difficult work of turning feminism into feminisms – something more representative of our wonderful variety'.[8]

In the twenty-first century, there has been a revival of feminism, led by young feminists around the world who are organizing online and offline. I was interested to see on my Twitter feed that in January 2014 the Feminist Wire was creating a new section called 'Personal Is Political'.[9] Perhaps it is on its way back – if it ever really disappeared.

But American critical theorist Nancy Fraser[10] argues that feminism today has gone down the road of the personal rather than the political, co-opted by an individualism that is intrinsically connected to capitalism. She believes that

> feminist ideas that once formed part of a radical worldview are increasingly expressed in individualist terms. Where feminists once criticised a society that promoted careerism, they now advise women to 'lean in'. A movement that once prioritised social solidarity now celebrates female entrepreneurs. A perspective that once valorised 'care' and interdependence now encourages individual advancement and meritocracy.[11]

Her analysis, explored further in the chapter on employment, shows clearly why it is so important for feminists to bring the link between the personal and the social back into an analysis that includes both as an integrated whole.

Feminism: a four-letter word?

But first we need to reclaim the word 'feminism'. To many people, it provokes strongly negative feelings, in a way that the term 'gender equality' does not. 'Patriarchy' has the same effect. They often provoke bewilderment and misunderstanding and even rage. And this is true for women as well as men.

British student Rose Kelly talks about her experience of the word 'feminism':[12]

> You'd think feminism was a four-letter word if you came to my campus. In a seminar a few weeks ago (about culture and diversity, by the way) the lecturer asked any feminists in the room to raise their hands. I'm ashamed to say that I didn't – in fact, only one girl in a class of 20 people did.
>
> I'm not embarrassed about what I stand for, far from it, but I'm reluctant to label myself a feminist because of the assumptions people jump to. Siobhan Garrigan, another British student, said: 'Young people don't want to identify as feminists because there is this man-hating, frumpy, lesbian image forced on us.'

Or Holly, from the Vagenda blog, writes: 'We asked girls why they thought feminism had become such a dirty word. The words that girls responded with were: "not sexy, unfeminine, angry, confusing, academic, intimidating, guilt-inducing, radical, scary, man-hating, exclusive, and not relatable".'[13]

Sri Danti Anwar, Secretary of the Ministry for Women's Empowerment and Child Protection in Indonesia, told me that: 'In Indonesia we don't want to label ourselves feminist – there is resistance to the word because it is seen as Western. Even the word gender we don't use all the time, we just paraphrase it. We have to relate the idea of gender equality to people's lives. That is the real challenge, not the language itself.'[14]

Some responses to the online survey for this book suggested changes to the word, but many young women are instead reclaiming it. For example: 'I think the feminist movement would attract more men if a more gender neutral term was used to describe it.'

After an era that many defined as 'post-feminist', it is heartening to see this new 'wave' of young women – and some young men – who are happy to call themselves feminists. Respondents in the online survey also said: 'I am inspired by the resurgence of feminism and feel immensely hopeful that it will effect real and lasting change.'

The younger generation may have different understandings of what that means from the older generation of feminists, but we would all subscribe to Rebecca West's definition that we do not want to be treated like doormats.

And although there has been much controversy around Caitlin Moran's book *How to Be a Woman*, its mixture of humour and challenge seems to have made many young women think about what it means to be female and feminist.[15] She says:

> here is the quick way of working out if you're a feminist. Put your hand in your pants.
>
> a) Do you have a vagina? and
> b) Do you want to be in charge of it?
>
> If you said 'yes' to both, then congratulations! You're a feminist.

Young Australian entrepreneur Holly Ransom agrees that her generation would rather not use the word 'feminist' but argues that this is 'because the evolution of the word has seen its mainstream connotation shift from "equal rights" to "hating men"'. If she uses the term 'equal rights', however, she says: 'I'm yet to meet a young woman who's not on board.' For Ransom, 'this is further proof of the need to raise the broader consciousness of the connotations of our language use and the framing of the current debate, as well as lifting the cloak of invisibility from the latent attitudinal and cultural phenomena that are currently serving as roadblocks to progress in gender equality'.[16]

Why do I need feminism?[17]

Young women at Duke University in the USA are among a number of groups who decided to set up what they called a 'PR campaign for feminism'. This is what they said: 'Our class was disturbed by what we perceive to be an overwhelmingly widespread belief that today's society no longer needs feminism ... We feel that until the denigration surrounding feminism and women's issues is alleviated, it will be hard to achieve total gender equality, both statistically and socially.'

Their account has now received more than four thousand photos from all over the world with statements about why feminism is needed. Most are from young women, a few from young men. This is a sample:

- 'I need feminism because in 1913 my great great grandmother gave her life in a Suffragette protest so that women could have the right to vote, and 100 years

Including men in feminism: the devil is in the detail

The involvement of men in campaigning for gender equality is not new, although it has always been a minority of men. In 1848, men attended the first women's rights convention in the Western world. In 1978, when men's groups proliferated in many countries, a statement issued in Los Angeles at the 5th National Conference on Men and Masculinities noted: 'the women's movement is the best thing that has ever happened for men'.

But there does seem to have been a change in recent years in the way that younger feminists view the involvement of men.

later, we STILL don't have equality between sexes.'
- 'I need Feminism because a 15 year old girl shouldn't have to come home so uncomfortable they're on the verge of tears, because a man has catcalled them in the street.'
- 'I need feminism because "men's jobs" (like engineering and physician) pay more than "women's" jobs. And that is NOT okay!'
- 'I need feminism because when I was a kid I told my family that girls couldn't be pretty and smart at the same time.'
- 'I need feminism because my nephew was called a "homo" (by his own father) for playing with the kitten I bought him. He's two years old.'
- 'I need FEMINISM because when talking about women's rights, someone came up to me and said, "Women are only good for keeping our stomachs full and our testicles empty."'

For example, UK Feminista[18] calls itself: 'A movement of ordinary women and men campaigning for gender equality', and though the 1,000-strong audience at its 2012 national conference were mainly women, it included a substantial minority of men. In addition, in the online research carried out for this book, 90 per cent of younger respondents said that men could be feminists, and 73 per cent of respondents over fifty.

Gary Barker, one of the pioneers of work with men from a gender equality perspective and a founder of Instituto Promundo in Brazil,[19] spoke to me of a 'generational shift':

There is a generation of young men who grew up with women's rights as daily reality, and a group of young women who expect nothing less than respect from men. I think that reality is driving our work in many parts of the world. There are more and more women who are women's rights advocates who say: 'Of course you (as men) should be here. You don't have to come and do your introductory remarks on why men should be part of gender. We get that.'[20]

Marisa Viana da Silva, a young feminist from Brazil, said:

In my experience, we as young feminists are more open to working with men than older feminists might be. We believe that men can also be feminists, and we are more flexible towards having these discussions. We recognize we need a wider movement and as much support as possible. Younger feminists have had a hard time accessing the more elite spaces older feminists have gained so we have to ask ourselves: how do we garner support and who do who work with? And that includes men. We need to work across different movements – in Latin America we are young feminists within the indigenous and environmental movements. You carry that identity with you wherever you go.[21]

I spoke to Andreas, a young man in Indonesia, who told me that because of education and changes in the law:

Women are now more willing to express their opinions and men are starting to hear them. Young educated men see that the women's movement should be supported. This is a change between generations. My father would raise his eyebrows and say 'What is feminism anyway?' and refer to the Bible, but in cities at least, younger men will support women.

In the villages it is still much more difficult – the head of the village and the family is the man, and the voice of women and girls in family decisions is not taken seriously.

On the website Feminism.com, American activist and feminist Amy Richards says in response to the question about whether feminism fights for the equality of both sexes:

I personally do fight for men's equality as much as I fight for women's – or rather fight to free men and women from inequalities. And those inequalities are based mostly on long-term stereotypes – i.e., that men are conditioned one way and women another. Feminism is about breaking down those assumptions and more and more scientific evidence backs that up – we are programmed in our genders. Men are often more punished for not conforming; women have been able to access male worlds more easily than men have accessed female worlds.[22]

Another reason why many young women are more welcoming to male feminists, however, may link back to American critical theorist Nancy Fraser's argument in Chapter 2 about individualization – because younger women tend to take a more individualistic approach that values choice above collectivism, there tends to be less opposition on political grounds to the choices that women make than there was for previous generations of feminists. A higher value is placed on individual choice than on political action.

Whatever the reasons that lie behind it, the fact that young feminists are more welcoming of men in their ranks is a big change.

In the past (and sometimes today), feminist or pro-feminist men were often attacked as representatives of the oppressors, of the patriarchy, as though everything that men have done to women is their personal fault, and as though men do not suffer from patriarchy as well. As writer and sociologist Allan Johnson notes, many people equate the word 'patriarchy' with 'men', but this is a misinterpretation of the word: 'Patriarchy is ... a kind of society in which men and women participate ... A society is patriarchal to the degree that it promotes male privilege by being *male dominated*, *male identified* and *male centred*. It is also organised around an obsession with control and involves as one of its key aspects the oppression of women.'[23]

Respondents in the online survey for this book noted: 'There do need to be women only spaces but there also needs to be spaces where men and women work together on these issues that affect both of them,' and 'In my experience some feminists are strongly against men becoming involved in feminist issues.'

Many feminists are suspicious of men wanting to get involved in something that has often rightly been a woman-only domain. They fear their motives, they are concerned that struggling women's groups will lose out once again to men in terms of both resources and attention. And they know that many groups calling themselves 'men's rights' are often misogynistic and woman-hating.

UK political anthropologist Andrea Cornwall and policy analyst Emily Esplen write in their paper on women's empowerment and men: 'As interest in men and masculinities has proliferated, so too has ambivalence amongst feminists about what this "men agenda" is all about. For some, it's a diversion from the real task of working with women to enable them to gain greater voice, agency and resources. For others, it's a nuisance and a threat, draining away vital funding and attention from women's rights. For others still, it's a fashion without political substance.'[24]

Putting it even more strongly in her response to Cornwall

and Esplen's article, Zimbabwean gender specialist Everjoice Win writes:

> All the things you suggest men should do; mobilizing other men, challenging one another, voting for women, working in trade unions, I agree they MUST do. Not as a favour to women. But because they want to, and they must do it if they are so called democrats, human rights activists/believers that they claim to be. The biggest thing men must do however is to change their personal behaviours, attitudes, and relationships with women. They must be consistent in demonstrating this change. We of course need EVIDENCE (yes that ever so wonderful word that they love throwing at us), that what they are doing is contributing to gender equality and women's enjoyment of rights. For now, please don't expect feminists to be jumping for joy because men have done what they should have always done. Be good people. Simple enough?

In fact, it is not that simple; we need to look at deeper cultural reasons. Young British writer Laurie Penny's take on this is interesting because she is able to pinpoint so clearly why even men who are not sexist and patriarchal benefit from patriarchy. Penny says:

> Of course not all men hate women. But culture hates women, so men who grow up in a sexist culture have a tendency to do and say sexist things, often without meaning to. We aren't judging you for who you are but that doesn't mean we're not asking you to change your behaviour. What you feel about women in your heart is of less immediate importance than how you treat them on a daily basis.
>
> You can be the gentlest, sweetest man in the world yet still benefit from sexism. That's how oppression works.

Thousands of otherwise decent people are persuaded to go along with an unfair system because it's less hassle that way. The appropriate response when somebody demands a change in that unfair system is to listen, rather than turning away or yelling, as a child might, that it's not your fault. And it isn't your fault. I'm sure you're lovely. That doesn't mean you don't have a responsibility to do something about it.[25]

Men also need to recognize not only that they benefit – sometimes even when they don't want to – from what is known as the 'patriarchal dividend', but also that there is a real danger that even the most pro-feminist men take up women's space – in meetings, for funding, in generally getting their voices heard. Melanie Judge, South African social commentator, told me: 'The way in which men engage must be under scrutiny because men who are activists claim a political space and have to be held to account in the ways in which they are engaging with masculinities and challenge or reproduce existing systems. They need to work with women on what is prevention – the devil is in the detail.'[26]

One respondent to the online survey for this book said:

To fully recognise women's oppression, to acknowledge that they benefit from it, even if not voluntarily and at last to not think they are the center of attention all the time. They mustn't steal our voices in our spaces. Their support is important I'm always glad when a guy identifies sexism on its own. However I'd like them to be more involved in their own deconstruction: like petitioning for paternity leave, try not to act like your typical male, etc. For once, I'd like the male gaze to be pointed at other guys and themselves.

And she has a point – in recent years, men working for gender equality have pushed for an end to violence against women, they have campaigned for better paternity leave and access to their children. But they have paid less attention to some of the issues around power and structural inequality that are central to the achievement of real equality between men and women.

Marc Peters, from the MenEngage Network, recognizes the alliances that are needed between those with privilege – white, Western, educated men like himself – and those without: 'When I step before a room of people to talk about equality, assumptions of my worldview abound based on my privilege. When I confound those expectations, I have no problem finding common ground and shared humanity with those who are systematically oppressed. Finding common ground with people like me, members of the oppressive group, is the challenge.'[27]

There are many young men like Marc who are doing just this – linking the personal and the political. They often face distrust and sometimes downright hostility when they attend meetings on gender or feminism, where they are the only man among thirty women. They cannot help but feel, on occasion, if not all the time, the representative of the enemy, the perpetrator, the one with the power, rather than the father, brother, uncle, grandfather, lover, partner, colleague or friend. The fact that they turn up despite this shows that they have as much interest in changing the status quo as many of the women in the room.

This takes courage. It is the kind of courage that women needed for so many years – and still need – when they are the only woman in the room. As feminists, this should be something that we can recognize.

Feminism, men and sexuality

In recent years, the LGBTI movement has made both feminists and men working on masculinities think again about how they define gender. MenEngage coordinator Oswaldo Montoya Telleria told me:

> There is a very profound link between the movement for men and gender equality and the LBGT movement. They are both challenging the status quo relating to homophobia. One of the main obstacles for men and masculinity is that we fear we might be under suspicion of not being heterosexual. The LGBT movement is challenging that norm – for them, diversity is the norm. I remember at the beginning of the 1990s in Nicaragua we created a movement of men against violence. Half the men were gay, half probably straight, some probably in between. We felt the patriarchal system harmed us and we wanted to support women's struggle. We were there together and we started confronting our fears and biases together. This was a very profound moment for me.

Masculinities expert and sociologist Michael Kimmel says that when he gives a lecture, there are always questions from what he calls 'angry-white-men-in-training'. In 'Who's afraid of men doing feminism?'[28] he gives one example: 'A burly white male student. Sitting in the back row, arms folded across his chest ... raised his hand: "What makes you such an expert on men?" he began. "The way you talk about listening to women, and supporting feminism, you must be a faggot or something. You sure aren't a real man."'

Kimmel goes on to say: 'No matter how many times I've been gay-baited, been rhetorically and literally called out, my manhood questioned, I'm still somewhat startled by it. Why would some people believe that supporting feminism is somehow a revelation of sexual orientation?' He goes on to answer his question: 'To the angry white men, profeminist men cannot exist, and so their

effort is to unmask me as a fraud of a man.' A man questioning traditional masculinities is somehow less of a man rather
than more of one. Which is why 'gay' is still an insult in many
school playgrounds, but one usually reserved more for boys
than for girls.

This is why it is so important for feminists – both male and
female – to incorporate an understanding of LGBTI issues into
their analysis, because LGBTI people are at the forefront of challenging traditional notions of gender: of what it 'should' mean
to be a man or a woman.

In some countries, including India, there is now a box labelled
'other' to tick as well as 'male' and 'female'. Those who do not
identify themselves as either sex are still 'other', but at least
they are a recognized category.

LGBTI people pay a high price for this challenge. In some
countries, tolerance of homosexuality is growing, while in others
LGBTI people are murdered, raped, imprisoned and even ex-
ecuted just for being who they are. Being gay is still illegal in
seventy-eight countries and being a lesbian is illegal in forty-nine.
In some countries in Africa, anti-gay legislation is being hotly
contested.[29]

Even in Europe, a 2013 poll found that 26 per cent of gay
people and 35 per cent of transgender people said they had
been attacked or threatened with violence during the past five
years. Almost half of the 93,000 surveyed said they had faced
discrimination or harassment on the grounds of their sexual
orientation, and half of these said they had not reported the
incident because 'nothing would change or happen anyway'.[30]

While in many countries in Latin America equal marriage
bills have been passed with little fuss, in France thousands of
pro and anti protesters took to the streets in 2013, and historian

Dominique Venner shot himself at the altar of Notre Dame cathedral in Paris because he objected so strongly to the idea.[31]

The links to right-wing movements are not coincidental; Marine Le Pen, leader of the right-wing National Front in France, tweeted about Venner's 'political gesture' in trying 'to wake France up'.[32] And many of those opposing gay marriage are also against feminism, and want a return to 'traditional' notions of what it is to be a man or a woman.

It is not only right-wing homophobic people and organizations who struggle with transgender issues. Feminists too, particularly radical feminists and those who focus on the unequal power relationships between men and women, have not always been welcoming to transgender women, because they are, or were formerly, male. Such groups have themselves been attacked by men's rights activists for excluding men.

In a statement in August 2013,[33] thirty-seven radical feminists from five countries acknowledged the oppression faced by members of the trans community, but noted that they believed changing gender identity was not a political solution, and is not a feminist strategy, and that potentially 'it undermines a solution for all, even for the transitioning person, by embracing and reinforcing the cultural, economic and political tracking of "gender" rather than challenging it ... Transitioning, by itself, does not aid in the fight for equal power between the sexes.'

Transgender people have been bitter about what they see as a betrayal. Another statement by feminist/'womanists'[34] in twenty-six countries affirmed their support for trans people and said that they were 'essential to feminism's mission to advocate for women and other people oppressed, exploited, and otherwise marginalized by patriarchal and misogynistic systems and people'. Supporters of transgender people within feminism have coined the term 'transfeminism', as one *Ms.* magazine blogger put it:

> Trans feminism ... is simply one of numerous third-wave feminisms that take an intersectional approach to challenging sexism and oppression. The only thing different about trans feminism is that it extends this feminist analysis to transgender issues, which have been largely overlooked or misinterpreted by feminists in the past ... When trans feminism is reduced to a debate about whether trans women 'count' as women or as feminists, it's a disservice not only to us but to feminism as a whole.[35]

I couldn't agree more.

Men's rights: feminists as 'agents of hate and corruption'

This next section looks at the men who are at the other end of the spectrum from most men in this book in that they support men's rights – often in opposition to women's rights. Their biggest guns seem to be reserved for feminists. One young female blogger writes about her friend Dan, who told her:

> I feel like 'feminism' is often used as a cloak for thinly veiled attacks on men. Many – not all – people who identify themselves as feminists seem to be self-serving and employ double standards. Feminism doesn't seem to be about equal rights any more. Women, legally speaking, have equal rights. Discrimination still exists but the feminist movement has moved to a point where the aim isn't equality, it's empowerment. They want to gain power and 'punish' men.[36]

There are also many men (and their female allies) who see feminism and women's rights as out to get the whole male sex. It doesn't seem to take much to bring out the fury, as the following examples show.

Take the rage directed against Caroline Criado-Perez in the UK. Her crime? A campaign in 2013 to have Jane Austen, a woman author, on British banknotes. She succeeded, but in the meantime she was hounded on social media with hundreds of rape and death threats. She has since deleted her Twitter account, claiming that she and other victims were let down by the police response 'not to feed the "trolls"'. 'Not feeding the trolls doesn't magically scrub out the image in your head of being told you'll be gang-raped till you die,' she said. 'What are victims meant to do with that image, the rage and the horror that it conjures up? We're meant to internalise it until it consumes us? Well, I'm sorry, but I'm not having that.'[37] The two people convicted were a man and a woman, showing once again that it is not just men who can be sexist.

Merely raising the issue of sexism can come at a high price. Anita Sarkeesian, a cultural critic working on an online video series titled *Tropes vs. Women in Video Games*, found when she started an online campaign in 2012 to raise money for her series that she faced a barrage of online harassment, including misogynistic messages and death threats. Some of her online critics even created a game where you could physically abuse an image of Sarkeesian. 'They weren't attacking my arguments,' she says. 'They were coming after me for merely proposing the idea that there's sexism in games.'[38]

In another example, when a group of sixteen-, seventeen- and eighteen-year-old young women at a school in the UK set up a Feminist Society and took photos of themselves with messages about why they needed feminism, the young men in their school subjected them to sexual objectification, vilification and harassment. The school's response? Not to track down and punish the men, but to ask the women to remove the photos 'because of concerns for their safety'. The young women said: 'The school's actions were a disservice to not only girls and women but to society at large. When we fail in supporting the voices of girls we also turn our backs on boys who need a helping hand in becoming more informed young men. Please join us in sending a message loud and clear to schools around the country that feminism belongs in education!' Many young women – and young men – responded. You can see their messages on the website.[39]

Those who attacked Caroline Criado-Perez and the boys who harassed the girls from the Feminist Society may not identify themselves as such, but they are part of a backlash against feminism that has been coming and going for at least fifteen years. It was explored in 1999 in writer Susan Faludi's *Stiffed: The Betrayal of the Modern Man*.[40] And in Hanna Roisin's *The End of Men and the Rise of Women* thirteen years later.[41]

Faludi interviewed American men from all walks of life. She notes that:

> A man controlling his environment is today the prevailing American image of masculinity. A man is expected to prove himself not by being part of society, but by being untouched by it, soaring above it ... And it is this very paradigm of modern masculinity – that it is all about being the master of your universe – prevents men from thinking their way out of their dilemma, from taking active political steps to resolve their crisis.[42]

In *The End of Men* Hanna Roisin announces that 'The tides have turned. The "age of testosterone" is decisively over. At almost every level of society women are proving themselves far more adaptable and suited to a job market that rewards people skills and intelligence, and a world that has a dramatically diminishing need for traditional male muscle.'

But others differ in fairly major ways as to how this change manifests itself. Warren Farrell, in his book *The Myth of Male Power*,[43] states that in fact it is women who are the 'winning' sex. It sets men against women – for example, he says: 'I look at how we have taken women's traditional area of sacrifice – raising children – and called it "sacrifice" while we have taken men's area of sacrifice – raising money – and called it "power".'

The website 'A Voice for Men' (AvFM)[44] goes even further. It states not only that it is: 'Pro Male – That means men and boys as a monolithic group, without consideration to race, creed, color, religion, lack of religion or sexual orientation. Racists, religious elitists or the anti-homosexual obsessed need not apply.' But that it is also 'Anti-feminist – AVfM regards feminism as a corrupt, hateful and disingenuous ideology based in female elitism and misandry. And AVfM regards all self-proclaimed feminists as agents, unwitting or otherwise, of that hate and corruption.' It also has a description of the Men's Rights Movement (MRM) as

> a grass roots, unfunded and loosely associated collection of human rights advocates focused on opposing the marginalization and vilification of men and boys in Western society. The MRM is a non-violent, non-political movement comprised of men and women who believe, based on a growing body of evidence that the human rights of males are being systematically removed by activists, lobbyists, politicians and academicians who cling to a misguided and wrongheaded belief that masculinity is fundamentally violent or harmful. This persistent myth is often referred to as cultural misandry.[45]

In fact, the 'A Voice for Men' website is articulating an anti-feminist message in exactly the way Susan Faludi outlined:

> Today it is men who cling more tightly to their illusions. They would rather see themselves as battered by feminism than shaped by the larger culture. Feminism can be demonised as just an 'unnatural' force trying to wrest men's power and control from their grasp. Culture, by contrast, is the whole environment we live in; to acknowledge its sway is to admit that men never had the power they imagined. To say that men are embedded in the culture is to say, by current standards of masculinity, that they are not men. By casting feminism as the villain that must be defeated to validate the central conceit of modern manhood, men avoid confronting powerful cultural and social expectations that have a lot more to do with their unhappiness than the latest sexual harassment ruling.[46]

These 'powerful cultural and social' expectations do need confronting. As we will see in this book, there are many ways in which men are doing 'worse' than women – they die younger, they commit suicide more often, they work long hours, they don't see their children. But in most ways, they are not. They fail to talk about power, about violence against women, about racism, sexism and unequal pay.

And by turning their fire on feminism, they miss the main point. That our current unequal society disadvantages men as well as women, and that men have much to gain from joining the feminist struggle rather than fighting against it.

Can men be feminists?

In accepting these facts, not all men have come to the conclusion that it is all feminism's fault. There are men who want to remove the straitjacket of traditional masculinity, and feel that this benefits all genders. Some of these may call themselves feminists, some pro-feminist. They are asking themselves the question posed by Susan Faludi: 'Why haven't men responded to the series of betrayals in their own lives – to the failures of their father to make good on their promises – with something coequal to feminism?'[47]

Oswaldo Montoya Telleria argues that they have, and that this provides a strong counter-position to the men's rights arguments: 'The problem is not women. They [the Men's Rights men] see themselves as separate from women. They see themselves as victims. They are victims of their own perceptions and under-standing of what is the problem, which is patriarchy.'[48]

One male respondent in the online survey for this book said: 'Male pride is a big thing. Men are brought up to think of themselves a certain way and that hurts them. Giving them more options as to what a man can be helps them enormously.'

These men who are working on gender equality and on their own attitudes to patriarchy – and they are a small, dedicated and slowly growing group – place themselves firmly in a pro-feminist camp. They are prepared to recognize that the personal is political; that this affects their own lives. They are prepared to change, and to talk to other men who may be more reluctant, about what those changes mean, from the mundane to the magnificent, from washing the dishes to equal pay.

But the online survey for this book also confirmed that there is still much disagreement about whether men can or should call themselves feminists. One respondent noted: 'I don't believe [men can be feminists] – feminism for me is about women's emancipation and that means women campaigning together. Men can and should support this but I fear if we claim to be feminists we risk diluting the message and worse still starting to assume control. Feminism offers men the chance to develop similar understandings about masculinity and what needs to change but this is in my view a parallel process not the same or competitive one.' And another: 'Only women can be feminists. Men can support feminists and feminist principles. It seems to me a matter of semantics whether a man can be a feminist but he can definitely be a pro-feminist man.'

Or as this South African man put it: 'I remember the first time someone suggested to me that work around gender was something men could do. It came as quite a surprise, like, "What?!" I'd always thought that was simply the domain of women, and perhaps I've even been defensive. But once it became clear that, no, this is in fact something that I can do and that I'm welcomed in doing, that was very helpful.'[49]

In a discussion with UK journalist Laurie Penny, writer Martin Robbins said: 'It's tough being a male feminist, albeit far less tough than being a female one. Some women argue that, as a man, I shouldn't be allowed to use the term to describe myself. There are men who say that I only support feminism to get laid ...'[50] And some men are evasive. British journalist Ally Fogg notes: 'The very notion of male feminism has never sat comfortably with me, and when I began writing and blogging more regularly on gender issues, it soon became apparent that it would be less troublesome for everyone if I did so from outside the feminist tent.'[51]

Likewise men's activist and director of the UK's Men's Network Glenn Poole: 'It's not that usual for men to talk about gender equality and those who do tend to come from a place of either pro-feminism or anti-feminism. The "isms" I prefer are optimism and activism.'[52]

Other men, however, are clear that they do call themselves feminists – and what this means to them. Dominic Hoey (aka Tourettes), poet, rapper, writer in New Zealand: 'I do call myself a feminist. I think anyone who believes in equality for both sexes is a feminist whether or not they use the title.' He believes that in fact it used to be easier for men to call themselves feminists than it is now:

> In the early '90s when I first was introduced to gender politics it was really acceptable for men to call themselves feminists, but now even a lot of woman are reluctant to use the term.
>
> I've always felt the gender roles we're assigned aren't always in our best interests, and are almost totally constructed. There's a really limited scope of acceptable behaviour and expression for men, and while it's not as extreme as that which women face it still has a hugely negative effect on both individuals and society as a whole. I believe these are feminist issues. Male privilege might benefit men on a superficial level but ultimately it represses both sexes.[53]

Worldwide, many men are joining the MenEngage Network,[54] an alliance of non-governmental organizations working together to promote gender equality. It believes that manhood is defined:

- by building relationships based on respect and equality,
- by speaking out against violence in your society,
- by having the strength to ask for help,
- by shared decision-making and shared power,
- and by how much you are able to respect the diversity and rights of those around you.

And manhood is not defined:

- by how many sexual partners you have,

BEYOND THE BINARIES | **41**

- by using violence against women or men,
- by how much pain you can endure,
- by how much power you can exert over others,
- or by whether you are gay or straight.

MenEngage has regional and country networks all over the world. Oswaldo Montoya Telleria says he believes that:

Gender equality is not only about gender but about all the other systems that need to be challenged at the same time – we are not just men and women, we have class, race, sexuality, religion ... I can connect with women's oppression because as a man from Nicaragua I know what it is to be seen as less than others. ... The connection between the personal and structural is key. Some of my colleagues privileged political work as the way of achieving change. But we also need grounding in the personal if we are to advance.

Equality and enlightenment: responses to the online survey for this book

I mentioned earlier that some men describe themselves as feminists and some as pro-feminists. But what do people working on feminism more generally think? Asked in the online survey 'can a man be a feminist?' 83 per cent said 'yes'.

There was a wide range of reactions, showing just how the debate is still very polarized:

- 'To be a "feminist" a man should support the objectives and campaigns of feminism/feminists, however men do not suffer oppression in the same way as women

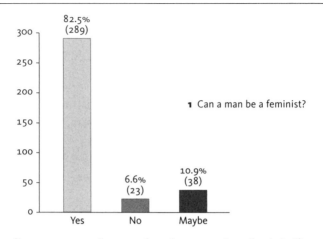

1 Can a man be a feminist?

(hence my preference for the term "profeminist"). Whereas overt public support of feminism by men is still limited, if a man works towards gender equality in the family, the community, at work, then he is likely to be a feminist or profeminist – although he may not accept either term.'

- 'I think it's unhelpful to use the title for men – it is too useful as a group identity for women – men can be supportive of feminist values but do not need to be encompassed in the term. It is politically valuable for women to be able to identify with the multiple feminisms as women.'

- 'Feminism should stop being seen as a term for just women. Feminism should include more men and not be women focused. We need men for gender equality, we need to change men's attitudes. It means for a man to have lost his own gendered constraints, to have lost gender binaries and to speak up against other men when they say negative comments or show bad behaviour towards women. Additionally for men to not call their children "wimps", or tell them to "man up" and allow them to be emotional and not see that as only allowed for girls and to not judge or make other men feel like less of a man if they're not into sports or are seen as "feminine".'

- 'To support the voices of women, to use his position of male privilege to give us a platform and let our ideas be spread more widely. To listen and learn from women and their work on gender, and to educate other men.'

- 'Same as for a white person to be non-racist or a person with no disabilities or illnesses to be fully inclusive with those with physical or mental disabilities or illnesses, or a straight person with LGBT people. Need to be continually aware of structural and historic inequalities, need to listen, to accept that their experience is a minor part of the narrative. Need to learn, and to act and to support and accept change.'

- 'One way of putting this is to say that: feminism is a tactic within a strategy for gender equality. A better way to think of it is probably not to think of feminism and gender equality as being different things at all. Inevitably, because bringing about change for women often means addressing imbalance between the genders, it can be fairly hard to isolate gender equality from feminism. So feminism for a man just means (or should just mean) being a gender egalitarian.'

- 'To want the best for his wife, daughter, mother. By definition he becomes a feminist.'

This respondent for the online survey noted: 'The feminist agenda has been good at telling men how not to behave, but is not so clear about how men should behave. What it means to be a man is something which men need to be involved in – women can be involved but ultimately men need to be the ones having these discussions.'

It is significant that many respondents felt that men could call themselves feminists. It seems clear that men need to have the kinds of discussions that women have had for so many years, about their role in society, about sexism and patriarchy, about how to prevent violence and to move forward both as men and with women. In the end, it doesn't really matter whether men call themselves feminists or pro-feminists or men for gender equality. What matters is that they are willing to take a stand against sexism, against violence and against stereotyping. As one respondent noted, the answer for both men and women is: 'Belief in equality. Simple as that.'

'Equality makes me happy': finding the sugar along with the medicine

Luis, a young man in a group I interviewed in El Salvador, one of the most violent countries in the world, said simply: 'Having more equality makes me happy. I am a better friend, with closer friendships with both boys and girls, and better conversations. I am more able to be trusted – because in our culture men are seen as those who deliver violence, trust is a difficult issue between the sexes.'[55]

Gender and masculinities expert Raewyn Connell from the University of Sydney notes that:

Gender equality is an undertaking for men that can be creative and joyful. It is a project that realizes high principles of social justice, produces better lives for the women whom men care about, and will produce better lives for the majority of men in the long run. This can and should be a project that generates energy, that finds expression in everyday life and the arts as well as informal policies, and that can illuminate all aspects of men's lives.[56]

But it is clear that, as Susan Faludi points out, this work is still confined to a relatively small group of men. Their numbers are growing, but there are still many challenges ahead. One of them, as Gary Barker recognizes, is that: 'men are going to have to give up privileges if they really want gender equality. Perhaps the hardest part to give up is the work that women and girls so often do for them,' and acknowledges that: 'we haven't done a good enough job of finding the sugar to go along with the medicine: helping men to understand that there are positive things that come with gender equality – better sex, happier partners, happier children, happier lives for men themselves because their children and their partners are happier'.[57]

Marc Peters from the MenEngage Network says that he calls himself a male feminist because 'the core of feminism is a belief that all people deserve to be treated fairly and justly regardless of gender identity. As a firm believer in the need for an equitable future for all people, there is no more natural affiliation for me.'[58]

Michael Kaufman, co-founder of the White Ribbon campaign of men against violence against women,[59] points out that men's power is contradictory:

Men enjoy social power, many forms of privilege, and a sense of often-unconscious entitlement by virtue of being male. But the way we have set up that world of power causes immense pain, isolation, and alienation not only for women, but also for men. This is not to equate men's pain with the systemic and systematic forms of women's oppression. Rather, it is to say that men's worldly power – as we sit in our homes or walk the street, apply ourselves at work or march through history – comes with a price for us. This combination of power and pain is the hidden story in the lives of men. It is men's contradictory experiences of power.[60]

Kaufman goes on to argue that feminism has shifted the fulcrum between men's power and men's pain as it questions patriarchy and notions of power – and that this is to the benefit of men as well as women.

Feminism as a movement for social change has won women a space in the world that they never had before. It continues to struggle with how and whether to include men. If feminists can find a way to move forward with the increasing numbers of men who are happy to find that common ground, this has the potential to change men's lives as well as women's – and to make our world a better place.

The next chapter looks at just how early our ideas of what it means to be male or female are shaped – and how these can be challenged.

3 | SHIFTING CULTURAL AND SOCIAL ATTITUDES

Becoming a better person …

'We had been married for eighteen years and I didn't know I was doing anything wrong,' said Anthony, who comes from Cape Town, South Africa. He continued:

A lot of men out there try to do their best to love their wives but it is difficult at times. I was impatient, I can see that now. If I asked Janine to come at three and she came five minutes later, I was angry. I never hit her, but I could look her dead. I would scream and shout if she said no to sex when I wanted it – I said it was God's will between a man and a wife. I come across a lot of men and most have the same problem. They go to work, and when they come back they press the remote. That is what most men are taught.[1]

Janine said: 'I used to be an assertive person but my relationship over the years had knocked my personality. I was at the point where I had moved out and we were heading for a divorce. It was affecting our girls too.'

It was at this point that Anthony decided to have counselling with Mosaic, a local women's organization. He said: 'One Christmas, I consulted God. I said "For my Christmas present, please put a smile on my wife's face." He answered me, but not in the way I had expected. I spoke to a friend and he sent me to a counsellor. She told me: "You don't just come here to help your wife, you come here to be a better person in society."'

Janine said she has seen a radical change in her husband's behaviour and it also changed her life:

> The programme empowered me to find myself again; to be Janine. Now when something happens we take five minutes' break. Anthony has become such a different person. He doesn't hassle me even over sex. We have become the best of friends. We talk; he cooks the nicest food ever. Roles have changed. I needed him to be a better man not just for me but for my children; to find a way to communicate with them. Now the girls are so loving to one another. They learn from Anthony. Things are so much better. I am not a nervous person any more.

And that change has been lasting: 'It has been three years since he finished the counselling and he is still a changed man. It has not just helped our relationship, it has helped him to respect women too.'

Anthony says: 'Since the counselling course, we still argue – Janine makes me cross almost every second day. But now I can walk away. That is how the counselling touched my life. Especially on Sunday, when all the dishes are dirty, I know it is our joint responsibility to clear up. So things are now a lot better between me and Janine. God answered my prayer that Christmas. He has put a smile on my wife's face.'

Janine and Anthony's story shows that it is possible for men to change. But also that it is not easy. This chapter is about the ways in which girls and boys, women and men, are taught to see each other and behave towards each other from a very early age. It examines the negative consequences of these attitudes for both sexes, and for LGBTI people. Girls, for example, may suffer from low self-esteem and violence, and have fewer opportunities and choices in life than their brothers. But conforming to ideas of what it is to be a 'real man' can stifle boys' emotions and lead to homophobia. The chapter examines how this plays out in different cultures, and how sex stereotyping is being reinforced by consumerism. It shows how pornography has played into sexist and discriminatory ways of viewing women. It looks at the influences of religious conservatism, and the importance of both men and women from within religions working for gender equality. Finally, it reveals the differences between generations – and gives examples of men and women who are showing a new way forward.

The chapter underpins the messages of the rest of this book about why it is so important to challenge these stereotypes, so that women can be freed up to achieve their potential and men can be liberated from narrow and constraining definitions of what it means to be a man – to the benefit of both sexes. Because that is what feminism is all about.

Everybody has a penis ... only girls wear barrettes

When Jeremy, aged four, decided to wear barrettes (hair slides) to nursery school, another little boy told Jeremy that he, Jeremy, must be a girl – because 'only girls wear barrettes'. Having parents who were trying to bring him up in a gender-neutral way, Jeremy tried to explain that 'wearing barrettes doesn't matter' and 'being a boy means having a penis and testicles'. Jeremy finally pulled down his pants as a way of making his point more convincingly.

The other child was not impressed and simply said: 'Everybody has a penis; only girls wear barrettes.'[2]

This story shows not only how confusing ideas about gender can be, but also how early attitudes about what it means to be male or female are shaped. British academic psychologist

Cordelia Fine writes: 'Cross-gender behaviour is seen as less acceptable in boys than in girls; unlike the term "tomboy", there is nothing positive implied by its male counterpart, the "sissy".' She notes: 'Parents were aware of the backlash their child might, or indeed had, received from others when they allowed them to deviate from gender norms.'[3]

Negative attitudes towards the female sex exist even before birth – sex-selective abortion and infanticide of baby girls in many countries has left at least 117 million girls missing from the world's population.[4] Today the problem has not improved. In China, this means that by 2020 there will be 30 to 40 million more young men than young women under nineteen. As *New Internationalist* magazine editor Vanessa Baird points out: 'That's equivalent to all the boys in the US.'[5]

Many cultures still prefer a son over a daughter. In India, for example, a mother gets more attention, special prayers and rest after having had a son than she does if she has a daughter.[6] In Ethiopia, a priest noted that: 'a baby boy gets seven ululations, while a baby girl gets only three'.[7] Proverbs show how deeply rooted these sentiments are. From Vietnam: 'One son is children, two daughters are none',[8] and from Nepal: 'To raise and care for a daughter is like taking care of somebody else's garden.'[9] Former US heavyweight boxing champion Muhammad Ali told an interviewer he had 'One boy and seven mistakes.'[10]

Children understand what it means to be male or female at a very young age. As one United Nations research report notes: 'By age five, most girls and boys have already internalized the gender role expectations communicated to them by their families, schools, the media, and society as a whole, and these norms will influence their behaviour and their development for the rest of their lives.'[11]

Plan International's 'State of the world's girls' reports, published each year since 2007, have shown the negative consequences of this for girls[12] – how they are valued less than their brothers, less likely to be sent to school, and more likely to have to carry out unpaid care work, with negative consequences for their studies. This fifteen-year-old from Nepal explains: 'I complete all the household tasks, go to school, again do the household activities and at night only I do my school homework. Despite all these activities, my parents do not give value or recognition to me. They only have praise for my brother, as he is the son.'[13] All this may mean that girls come to feel inferior and lack self-esteem – and that boys also see them like this.

A study on early childhood in India confirms these roles: 'The role of the girl child is to be a demure, accommodating, and respectful homemaker. A "good" girl of six is one who listens to and respects her adults, helps mother in household chores, and one who stays and plays at home.'[14]

Puppy dog tails

The way that boys are taught to view girls and women strongly influences their attitudes and behaviours as they grow up. And the way boys are viewed can be equally a stereotype, as this traditional British nursery rhyme makes clear:

What are little boys made of?
Snakes and snails,
And puppy dog tails,
That's what little boys are made of.

A report on masculinities by the Women's Commission for Refugee Women and Children notes that: 'Young boys ... are generally allowed more freedoms and have fewer restrictions placed on them than young girls. They are taught to play rough, to stand up for themselves, not to walk away from a fight. They run out to play while their sisters are kept indoors to care for younger children and to help with domestic chores.'[15] And in India: 'A "good" boy is expected to be naughty, to have many friends to play with (outside the home), and not always listen to parents.'[16]

Not surprising, then, if boys from an early age refuse to help with childcare or work in the home, because they are taught that this is 'women's work'. For example, twelve-year-old Dibaba's mother in Ethiopia says her son complains when he is asked to look after his younger siblings: 'He says, "Why is it only me who should care for the baby? Do you think that I am a girl?" He says, "You should recognise I am a boy." He says, "Let the girls carry the children."'[17] In Gihogwe, Rwanda, focus groups of boys aged twelve to fourteen said: 'The majority of men fear to do home activities because they think they will be laughed at.'[18]

'Traditional practices included a tendency to privilege boys – giving boys wider leeway in behaviour, and excusing non-social behaviours by saying "boys will be boys",' says one report by the Consultative Group on Early Childhood Care and Development. But 'this does not teach boys responsibility, nor clarify what will be expected of them. When they are asked to take on responsibilities in their adult life, in increasingly complex contexts, they have little support or preparation for the task.'[19]

For boys, this lack of options can lead to risky behaviours such as smoking, drinking and violence; what anti-violence campaigner Jackson Katz calls 'The Tough Guise': 'an extreme notion of masculinity that emphasizes toughness and physical strength and gaining the respect and admiration of others through violence or the implicit threat of it'.[20] This also denigrates anything female, with serious effects on relationships between men and women, and on views of LGBTI people.

A respondent to the online survey for this book noted that:

> socialisation is probably the biggest causal factor [in preventing men becoming involved in gender equality], as it causes a blindness to the experiences of women and creates the illusion of equality – in the same way that white people are often blind to their privilege in society. I don't believe men are unable to express emotions – they express plenty in my experience – although I believe men are actively discouraged from displaying certain emotions (vulnerability, fear, sorrow) which society portrays as weak in men and natural in women.

Pink stinks

One factor which clearly reinforces the stereotypes at an early age in most of the Western world – and increasingly in some of the South as well – is the billion-dollar[21] market for children's toys, books and clothes.

Pink for girls and blue for boys is sold as being hard-wired into our genes in the West. But in fact, it was only 100 years ago that pink was seen as suitable for boys rather than girls. In June 1918, the *Ladies' Home Journal* in the USA noted that pink was a boy's colour because it was stronger than blue, which was considered 'more delicate and dainty, prettier for the girl'.

This is, as you may have noticed, no longer the case. For maybe the past decade or so, little girls have inhabited a universe that is, almost entirely, pink. 'There's been', says Abi Moore, a thirty-eight-year-old freelance television producer in the UK, 'a wholesale pinkification of girls. It's everywhere; you can't escape it. And it needs to change. It sells children a lie – that there's only one way to be a "proper girl" – and it sets them on a journey, at a very, very early age. It's a signpost, telling them that beauty is more valued than brains; it limits horizons, and it restricts ambitions.'

The pink-and-blue divide seems to have become worse in the past few years. Many stores now divide their catalogues and their shops very clearly into 'boys' and 'girls'. Finding a toy or a coat that does not conform to the stereotype is extremely difficult.

There is nothing inherently wrong with girls – or boys – wearing pink. What is objectionable is the targeting of children and their parents with such gender stereotypes for both boys and girls, which will have consequences for the kind of adults they will become, and how they relate to the opposite sex and how they bring up their own children if they have them. As this father of two small girls, aged three years and eight months, noted: 'I am frustrated by my constant struggle to find toys and, more importantly, literature, beyond the realms of princesses and fairies (all of whom seem only interested in finding a prince, wearing dresses and getting married).'[22] If you try to find clothing for a baby but don't know its sex, the task today is almost impossible.

Moore launched an anti-pink (or rather pro-some-alternatives-to-pink) campaign with her twin sister Emma, a senior voluntary sector worker. The campaign, PinkStinks, started out with the aim of offering girls alternative role models. Trying to reverse the seemingly unstoppable tide of pink was simply another way, they felt, of challenging what they saw as rampant and unacceptable gender stereotyping, from earliest childhood.

PinkStinks has since featured in television and newspaper reports in twenty-two countries around the world, from Argentina to South Africa. 'People say it's all innate – they think we're attacking something natural, within them,' says Abi Moore. 'But there are tremendously powerful forces out there. This is about money and marketing. That's worth challenging, isn't it?'[23]

And some children are doing just that. In December 2008, a class of children in Sweden noticed the Christmas Toys R Us catalogue had pages of pink for girls and pages of superheroes for boys. Ebba Silvert, aged thirteen, said: 'I think that girls can be superheroes if they want to, they don't have to look like small little princesses. The boys were action and fighting and stuff and the girls were sitting at home and being cute.'

Together with her friend Philippe Johansen, Ebba wrote a letter to the advertising ombudsman and to Toys R Us. On 9 October 2009 the ombudsman reprimanded Toys R Us. They found that out of 58 pages of toys there were only 14 where boys and girls were pictured together with the same toys. On 44 pages girls or boys were playing separately.

Ebba says: 'The Toys R Us Christmas catalogue has to change for next year. It made me feel very proud that we succeeded and I am very happy I learned that you can make a difference even if it seems impossible.'[24]

PinkStinks also ran campaigns against the children's toy store the Early Learning Centre (ELC) – which I remember as a place where you could buy fascinating toys to help children learn that had nothing to do with their gender. The PinkStinks website noted:

Whilst the ELC refused to acknowledge the issues, a year later their Christmas catalogue had evident changes. This included a reduced use of the word 'pretty' to describe toys/dressing-up clothes for girls and a marked increase in the number of girls dressed in outfits other than 'princess'. Boys and girls feature playing together with toy kitchens and there are other subtle differences.[25]

Other campaigns against the gender stereotyping of toys are also having some success: 'Let toys be toys',[26] a parent-led campaign in the UK, found in their 2013 pre-Christmas survey that there had been a 60 per cent reduction in the use of 'Girls' and 'Boys' signs in stores. The campaign notes: 'From inflatable pink orcas and Boutique monopoly to pink superman costumes and pink glue (we kid you not!) the idea of taking a regular product, giving it a pink makeover and selling it back to girls is so common that one wonders how girls will cope when they grow up and find out that the world is *not* covered in pastel pink.'[27]

Perhaps one project in El Salvador can show a different way forward. I visited one nursery in Cabañas, in northern El Salvador, where the teachers were trying to find ways to challenge gender stereotypes even with the tiniest children.

Red beans and hard hats[28]

Samuel has put on a blue apron to protect his clothes and is standing at the stove cooking a yellow pot full of beans. He carefully fills the pot from another metal container and then shakes the beans so they will not burn. This will be *frijoles refritos* (a dish of cooked and mashed beans), he tells me.

Samuel is not a famous chef or – yet – a man who likes cooking. But he probably has more chance of being either of these than his father or brothers.

Because Samuel is only four. He attends a nursery in Cabañas, in northern El Salvador. He is lucky – nursery

---

provision in El Salvador is minimal; 1.8 per cent of children from birth to three and 57 per cent of those from four to six attend any kind of nursery.[29] And this is not just any nursery, but one of fifty-six in the country that are trying to promote gender equality from an early age. 'People don't understand the importance of providing early years services – we believe that we can challenge the stereotypes of what it means to be a boy or a girl by providing different possibilities in our nurseries,' says Beatriz de Paúl Flores, from Plan International.

Together with Salomon Cruz, in charge of Plan's education work, Beatriz designed a gender-equal programme for the 'Centro Bienestar Infantil' (Early Years Wellbeing Centre). The programme is new; it has only been running for two years, and Beatriz notes that it is 'a slow process, that needs to be sustained through time'. It was surprisingly difficult to find books and films that did not stereotype boys and girls, toys that were not just pink and blue or designated only for one sex, and dolls with realistic shapes and genitalia.

Beeri Yem Sanchez Rivera, one of the teachers in the centre, says she came to this nursery because 'I wanted to learn more about gender, about how to help girls and boys relate better and to accept themselves and accept others.'

The programme also works with parents so that they understand what the nursery is trying to do. For example, they talk about non-sexist language and discuss the ways that boys and girls are expected to behave. Beatriz says they meet little resistance, although it is easier to get mothers than fathers to attend the meetings. 'The parents see that we also teach children to behave, to eat their food, to relate well to each other. They see the benefits of early years education,' says Alexia, a teacher in the school. 'The fathers see that the boys talk to the girls with more respect and that both boys and girls can share toys and spaces and play together. They see this as a positive thing.'

Beatriz says she recognizes that outside influences also shape children's attitudes, so the project also wants to work with the government to look at the school curriculum. They are already training people and institutions such as the Government's ISNA (Instituto Salvadoreño para el Desarrollo Integral de la Niñez y la Adolescencia – Institute for the Integral Development of Children and Adolescents) in gender and early education and working with them on a national gender policy for early years.

Samuel, after a period of banging drums with his friend, has now moved on to feeding a baby doll. Next to him, Fatima, in a sparkling white doctor's coat, is listening to Valeria's heartbeat through a stethoscope. She has an expression of concentration on her face and Valeria gazes trustingly up at her. Most of the children come from poor families; Valeria is much smaller than her peers and it has taken her some time to adapt to the nursery but she has made huge progress in the past months, says Beeri.

Of course, some little boys still want to wear hard hats and bang hammers and be builders or truck drivers and the girls still want to dress as princesses, but in this nursery it is acceptable for the children to try out whatever roles they feel comfortable with. However, in a country with a strong tradition of machismo and high levels of violence, it will be interesting to see whether their grounding at this early stage of their lives will mean that Fatima and Samuel and their friends will be able to forge the beginnings of a more equal and violence-free society.

Ed Mayo, co-author of *Consumer Kids: How Big Business Is Grooming Our Children for Profit*, argues that the children's market has now reached the stage where 'it's no exaggeration to talk of a gender apartheid'.[30]

Challenging these stereotypes is essential, because by categorizing toys as 'boys only' or 'girls only', we are teaching children a very narrow definition of what it means to be a man and a woman, one that reinforces traditional views of both and limits the possibilities of wider choices.

Big boys should cry

One of the strongest messages still given to boys today, even at a very young age, is: 'Big boys don't cry.' Messages about what it means to be a man begin at a very young age. As American masculinities expert Jackson Katz notes:[31] 'Boys and young men learn early on that being a so-called 'real man' means you ... have to show the world only certain parts of yourself that the dominant culture has defined as manly.' He goes on to cite a list of what young men themselves define as being the qualities of a 'real man':

- A real man is physical.
- Strong.
- Independent.
- Intimidating.
- Powerful.
- In control.
- Rugged.
- Scares people.
- Respected.
- Hard.
- A stud.
- Athletic.
- Muscular.
- A real man is tough.

And what is the worst insult for boys if they don't measure up? They are called a girl. Or gay. Or some variation of both.

In another survey by Instituto Promundo and the International Center for Research on Women on men and gender equality in six countries,[32] 86 per cent of men in India and 85 per cent of men in South Africa agreed that 'to be a man it is important to be tough'. This compared with 62 per cent in Croatia, 44 per cent in Brazil, 38 per cent in Chile, 19 per cent in Rwanda and only 8 per cent in Mexico.

Being tough also means not talking about your emotions. And that too is the stereotype associated with boys; that they are silent, and that friendship is often about doing things together and talking about this rather than talking about what they think or feel.

However, Niobe Way's research has found something quite different. Way is a professor of Applied Psychology at New York University, and she and her team have interviewed hundreds of teenage boys for her book *Deep Secrets: Boys' friendships and the crisis of connection.*[33]

She notes that cultural ideas of masculinity promote competition and autonomy as ideals for boys, but in fact most of the hundreds of boys that she and her research team interviewed valued their male friendships and 'saw them as essential components of their health, not because their friends were worthy opponents in the competition for manhood but because they were able to share their thoughts and feelings – their deepest secrets – with these friends'.

What Way and her team also found, however, was that at around the age of fifteen or sixteen, this starts to change. As Mohammed, one of the boys in the study, said: 'Recently ... you know I kind of changed something. Not that much but you know I feel like there's no need to – I could keep [my feelings] to myself. You know, I'm mature enough.' But he also begins to speak in the same year for the first time of being depressed and isolated. The consequences of this, in terms of suicide and violence, are explored further in Chapter 7.

There are other harmful effects of this repression for boys. Psychologist Joseph Pleck from the University of Illinois in the USA surveyed 1,880 young men between the ages of fifteen and nineteen and found that those who believed in and practised what they saw as traditional masculinity reported a more adversarial view of relationships between women and men, more sexual partners in the last year, a less intimate relationship during last intercourse with their most recent partner and less consistent use of condoms – all factors harmful not only to the young men but to their partners as well.[34]

The causes are clear. They relate directly to the way that boys are socialized to be men. And these are not hard-wired into boys from the start. Lise Eliot, associate professor in the Department of Neuroscience at the Chicago Medical School, points out in her book *Pink Brain, Blue Brain* that 'infant brains are so malleable that small differences at birth become amplified over time, as parents, teachers, peers and the culture at large unwittingly reinforce gender stereotypes ... Girls are not naturally more empathic than boys, they are just allowed to express their feelings more.' In the same way: 'boys are empathetic and can learn to be even more so if we don't exaggerate stereotypes and try to focus on their emotional development as much as their athletic and academic skills'.[35]

Masculinities expert Michael Kaufman told me about a project in Canada that wanted to teach pre-adolescent boys about parenting and help them develop greater empathy. He said:

> A group of parents and teachers took the boys to a nearby childcare centre. There were protests by the boys that this was for girls. But they were forced to go and, once there, quickly became interested in the babies they were taught to hold. The second week, when they returned, the first thing that each boy said was 'Where's MY baby?' It hadn't taken long for the boys to form an emotional attachment to the baby they had played with for only an hour the previous week.

Marcio, from Rio de Janeiro, Brazil, is one man who made that change to being able to show his emotions. In a film for the MenCare campaign,[36] he talks about always dreaming of being a father, and of how his own father was violent and womanizing and never there for him. What made him change was joining a group of other men to talk about their fathers and what fatherhood meant to them. He says:

> There is a saying that goes if you don't put old things outside

you can't put new things inside ... at first [in the group] I didn't talk. I was locked away where no one could reach me. But being with others and hearing their stories, it helped me overcome the past. Things I could absorb from other fathers ... a lot of what I believed about fatherhood changed. And finally I opened up. Bad things left me and good things came in.

Marcio also talks of how his father's behaviour was just what was 'expected', because he was a man. Challenging this – not being seen as 'tough', or being different, for example being homosexual, or transgender – can mean that boys and men still face ostracization or even violence, even at a young age, as Phillip's story shows.

Phillip's story

Phillip's mother Jane tells how from an early age he faced taunts from his peers in his school in Britain.

My son's journey through the education system: at the age of three, a rather sweet, ever smiling little boy, entered a world that for years would result in him experiencing rejection from many of his peers, and the reason was ignorance.

Phillip experienced his first bullying at nursery school with taunts of 'girl' and physical violence. The hurt, confusion and tears he shed were simply heartbreaking. I might add that Phillip was always taller by a year than his actual age; hence 'girl' could only have been due to his gentleness. Phillip went on to primary school, where he still had to endure taunts of 'girl' and some violent attacks. Phillip recalls this time as when he realized how nasty people could be. Phillip remained gentle and kind, so as a mother the pain he suffered was unbearable. By late juniors I knew my son was different, I was already thinking much about his sexuality.

Within weeks of starting secondary school the homophobic remarks began with taunts of 'queer' and 'girl'. Phillip suffered a physical attack resulting in a black eye. This attack resulted in Phillip too receiving a detention, and appallingly, the teacher from the class it happened in told Phillip the incident was 'the highlight' of his day! Year 8 Phillip recalls as awful, the 'gay' and 'queer' taunts became more frequent, people regularly stole his belongings. I made sure he knew he could walk out if he couldn't cope. During this year he was punched in the eye for not touching a picture of a vagina. As a parent I spent every day scared for his welfare. After complaints to the school I informed them any more physical attacks would be reported to the police.

By year nine he'd formed some good friendships that lightened his life, giving him much-needed support. Fortunately some of his friends were also gay. These friends supported him through the gay taunts. This continued until the end of year 10; during one of many verbal attacks from a group of boys, they asked 'Are you f***ing queer?' Phillip replied 'YES'. They were shocked and said 'really?' and 'you are all right really'. He became everyone's favourite gay; his peer group finally left him alone.

During all this time I wrote letters regarding my child's

welfare to the school. They assured me they would try to help, but at no time was the homophobic intimidation challenged. Against all odds Phillip worked very hard, he now attends college.

Since leaving school Phillip has suffered three assaults, each time by gangs of lads out gay-bashing. Each attack resulted in hospital treatment, including stitches to repair his mouth.[37]

The inherent contradictions between homophobia and traditional masculinities are clear. Questions around homophobia in four countries found that the number of men who said they would be 'ashamed' to have a gay son ranged from 43 per cent in Brazil, 44 in Chile, 63 in Croatia to 93 per cent in India.[38] Of course, this can be true for mothers too, who are equally tied into patriarchal views of what a man 'should' be. The word 'gay' continues to be used as an insult for boys in school playgrounds around the world.

In the online survey for this book, respondents generally felt people were becoming more tolerant of homosexuality – although this too was qualified by region, as one respondent noted: 'In Africa especially, tolerance of homosexuality has gone down. This needs to be addressed urgently. We see homophobia as also linked to gender-based violence.' In Africa, thirty-seven countries have legislation against homosexuality, and new anti-gay laws in countries such as Uganda, Nigeria and Russia have high levels of support from both women and men, linked to religion and the upholding of 'culture' as well as views of masculinity.[39]

In the USA, a 2013 survey of LGBT Americans found that 92 per cent felt that in the past ten years society has become more accepting of LGBT people and they hope this will continue to improve. However, 58 per cent also say they have been the target of jokes or slurs, 39 per cent say that 'at some point in their lives they were rejected by a family member or close friend because of their sexual orientation or gender identity', and 30 per cent say they have been physically attacked or threatened.[40] Katz links this violence back to traditional masculinities once again:

> I think a lot of violence is as a result of men and boys compensating for not being big and strong and muscular. So in other words, if you're a young guy, 16 or 17 years old, but you don't look like Arnold Schwarzenegger and you want people to respect you on a bodily level and your definition of respect involves physical strength and physical respect, what can you do? Well one thing you can do is you can pack a Glock and all of a sudden your friends are backing up from you. All of a sudden you're a man.[41]

Body image

Looking like Schwarzenegger – or in fact an even more muscled version – has become even more of an aim for young men today than it was ten or fifteen years ago. Masculinities expert Michael Kaufman, in a talk in South Africa in June 2013, compared the superheroes of the past with those of today. Spiderman or Superman or Batman used to have bodies that today would be considered almost flabby. In 2013, the same heroes are almost impossibly muscular, with small waists and huge pecs. This is particularly true of video games, where women are either impossibly large-breasted or slim-waisted – or are simply there as victims or cyphers. 'There are not very many female protagonists that lead their own games,' says Anita Sarkeesian, a cultural critic working on an online video series entitled *Tropes vs. Women in Video Games*. 'And when you do have a female lead, it's often in full-body third person and they're highly sexualized.'[42]

Not surprising, then, that women and girls – and also men and boys, though this is less openly discussed – have a range of disorders that relate to their body image. The American Psychological Association's Task Force on the Sexualization of Girls has noted its concern about the negative effects of a more sexualized culture on girls, including cognitive functioning, physical and mental health, sexuality and attitudes and beliefs.[43] Which was why Deborah Tolman and Lyn Mikel Brown set up SPARK (Sexualization Protest: Action, Resistance, Knowledge).[44] SPARK is run by girls and aims to 'reject the sexualized images of girls in media and support the development of girls' healthy sexuality and self-esteem'.

It is much needed. Activist Michael Koschitzki told *Der Spiegel* that 'a real woman with Barbie's figure would be anorexic, wouldn't be able to walk, and would never get her period'. The *Huffington Post* reported how, following on from this, illustrator Nickolay Lamm put together a Barbie 'based on what she would look like if she had normal measurements. In comparison, when scaled up to human size, Barbie dolls would have unhealthy measurements of an 18" waist, 33" hips and a 36" bust compared with the typical 19-year-old girl's 31" waist, 33" hips and a 32" bust. The measurements have been taken from the CDC (Centres for Disease Control and Prevention) measurements of the average 19-year-old American girl.'[45]

Young women today suffer from a range of bodily related disorders, including obesity and anorexia. One study in the UK found that: 'One in three girls aged eleven are overweight' and 'among 16–24-year-olds, twice as many young women as young men are seriously obese'. It also points out that: 'Obesity has a direct link with poverty and social exclusion.'[46]

In one study in thirty-five countries, mainly in the West, 25 per cent of eleven-year-old girls and 40 per cent of fifteen-year-olds thought they were too fat.[47] The same study found that in Japan one in twenty girls in high school in Tokyo and in Canada one in four teenage girls has symptoms of anorexia, which can lead to premature osteoporosis, lack of menstrual periods, exhaustion and even death. Amanda, aged nineteen, said: 'I don't think I could pinpoint one thing that makes me happy about being anorexic. I suppose it makes me feel special in a way, that it's something not everybody can have, and that I have more control over myself than everybody else.'

There is much less recognition that boys and young men can suffer from body-related disorders too. Jenny Langley, a mother with an anorexic son in the UK, spoke of her isolation in a book written for other parents in her situation:[48] 'how many incidences of male anorexia have you heard of? Certainly until my son was afflicted, I hadn't heard of any examples. As it turned out, neither had my GP, or any of the teachers at my son's school or any of my friends or work colleagues. So it was a huge shock when my 12 year old son started to disappear before my eyes ...' She goes on to describe the swift onset of the illness and his gradual recovery, a pattern known to many parents of anorexic girls.

Pornography: making sexism sexy

In the online survey for this book, a number of respondents, both men and women, mentioned increased sexualization of girls and pornography as something that they felt was leading to a deterioration in women's rights. These included: 'Sexualisation of girls. The negative impact of Internet porn on sexual relationships'; 'I can see social attitudes particularly swinging back towards the political right, and the onward march of global capitalism has normalised the commodification of human sexuality, particularly via pornography, which can definitely be seen in relationships and interpersonal gender relationships'; 'I'm thinking about particularly the acceptability of porn watching, going to strip clubs, thinking women just don't have a sense of humour if they don't find it ok and funny – before it was all a bit sordid and shameful and lots of men wouldn't admit to enjoying that kind of exploitation.'

Perhaps the most shocking thing about the increase in pornography now that it is so readily available on the internet is just how violent and demeaning of women the majority of it is.

For example, a content analysis in the USA of fifty best-selling adult videos found that:[49]

- Nearly half of the 304 scenes analysed contained verbal aggression.
- Over 88 per cent showed physical aggression.
- 72 per cent of aggressive acts were perpetrated by men.
- 94 per cent of these acts were committed against women.
- Fewer than 5 per cent of the aggressive acts provoked a negative response from the victim, including flinching and requests to stop.

This pornographic 'reality' was further highlighted by the relative infrequency of more positive behaviours, such as verbal compliments, embracing, kissing or laughter.[50]

There is evidence, too, that pornography has a direct impact on men's views of women, and also reinforces stereotypes across the board in terms of class, profession, race, etc. 'Unlike real life,' says Edward Marriott, 'the pornographic world is a place in which men find their authority unchallenged and in which women are their willing, even grateful servants. "The illusion is created," as one male writer on pornography puts it, "that women are really in their rightful place and that there is, after all, no real and serious challenge to male authority."'[51]

One Australian study found a clear link between viewing porn and young people's attitudes towards relationships.[52] It found that violence, very rough sex and even rape are seen as 'normal' by children and adolescents viewing porn. Michael Flood, a masculinities expert who carried out the study, says:

> There is compelling evidence from around the world that pornography has negative effects on individuals and communities ... porn is a very poor sex educator because it shows sex in unrealistic ways and fails to address intimacy, love, connection or romance. Often it is quite callous and hostile in its depictions of women. It doesn't mean that every young person is going out to rape somebody but it does increase the likelihood that will happen.[53]

Bill Margold, a star of the porn industry (and also a men's rights activist), was quite open about the way that porn was a way for men to 'get even': 'My whole reason for being in this industry is to satisfy the desire of the men in the world who basically don't care much for women and want to see the men in my industry getting even with the women they couldn't have when they were growing up. So we come on a woman's face or brutalise her sexually: we're getting even for lost dreams.'[54] Ray Wyre, a therapist who worked with sex offenders, said: 'The very least pornography does is make sexism sexy.'[55]

There is also strong evidence that porn also affects sexual relationships, especially for young people. One study noted: 'Men who consume pornography may expect their partners to occupy traditional female roles and be less assertive.'[56] Another found that 'Youth who look at violent x-rated material are six times more likely to report forcing someone to do something sexual online or in-person versus youth not exposed to x-rated material.'[57]

Not only does most pornography depict women as there solely for male pleasure – and often violent pleasure – but they are hairless and thus disturbingly infantilized. One direct result of this is that younger women now shave or shape their pubic hair. Another is the rise in plastic surgery, linked not just to 'perfect' bodies seen in porn, but to the airbrushed and Photoshopped women seen on every billboard, in every magazine, television or music video. A study in Sweden found that young people who frequently viewed pornography were more likely to engage in anal sex, group sex and casual sex than those who did not.[58]

As for the effect on men, American feminist author Jessica Valenti notes that:

Internet porn and the normalisation of pornography have spawned a whole new generation of guys who were raised thinking that porn sex equals normal sex. Not to mention a whole generation of girls who think porn sex is the only way to please guys ... Young men in the US have been brought up to think that they have open access to women's bodies and sexuality. Everything in American culture tells men that women are there for them, there for sex, constantly available.[59]

Debates about, and resistance to, this 'pornification' have

often been led by, or are between, feminists and other women. Not surprisingly perhaps, few men have dared to intervene. Matt McCormack Evans is an exception. He is a young man in the UK who started a campaign against porn called antipornmen.org.

Young men who hate porn[60]

It was in the cerebral setting of a university library that Matt McCormack Evans noticed how pornography was shaping his life. He was watching a female librarian stack books on shelves, stretching for the highest recess, when it occurred to him he 'should look up some librarian-themed porn that evening,' he says. 'I remember making that mental note, and then catching myself.'

McCormack Evans was 20 at the time, and he had been using pornography regularly for a year or so, since starting university and having private access to a computer. At first, he didn't think this was a problem. It was something he did alone; no one had to know. The habit need never bleed beyond his student bedroom. Then he realised his male peers were using porn too, openly, frequently – almost celebrating it – and it started to make him feel uncomfortable.

He had glimpses of how it might influence their lives. There was the librarian moment: a flash of how porn might shift the way he responded to women in the real world. There was the moment he noticed a male friend struggling not to ask the stupid, inappropriate question about oral sex that had occurred to him when a female friend mentioned her sore throat.

McCormack Evans, a thoughtful, articulate young Londoner, was a philosophy student at Hull University in the northeast of England, and he had never been part of a particularly laddish crowd, but he noticed that the 'relatively well-rounded young men' he knew were changing.

'They came to uni, got their first computer, were alone a lot, and everyone became much more laddish. It got to the point where someone groped a woman's bum in a club, and I completely flipped out.'

McCormack Evans, now 22, has just co-founded an online project to get men talking about their use of porn. Other such projects have often come from a religious standpoint but the Anti-Porn Men Project is grounded in feminist principles, in the notion that pornography is an important social issue and has a bearing on violence perpetrated against women and wider inequalities.

In setting up the site, McCormack Evans is one of the few men worldwide to discuss publicly pornography from a feminist perspective – positive about sex itself, open to the idea of people engaging in the widest range of consensual sex acts, but concerned about the industrialisation of sex and where this leads.

The influence of culture and religion

Another attack on feminism and gender equality that relates to attitudes comes from a completely different end of the spectrum, and that is religious conservatism. Egyptian feminist Nawal el Saadawi said in an interview that she believes religious extremism is the biggest threat to women's liberation today. 'There is a backlash against feminism all over the world today because of the revival of religions,' she says. 'We have had a global and religious fundamentalist movement.'[61]

A survey by the Association of Women's Rights in Development of 1,600 women's rights activists in 160 countries found that eight out of ten activists thought religious fundamentalisms have had a negative impact on women's rights. They cited more than six hundred examples of how this 'manifested in the control over women's bodies, sexuality, autonomy, freedom of movement and participation in public life'.[62]

Religious conservatives often seek to reaffirm traditional notions of masculinity and femininity, driving women back into the home and ensuring that men are in charge. As Pat Robertson, an American Christian televangelist, said to one man: 'You're supposed to be a leader, you're supposed to be the high priest. You're supposed to intercede for your family before the Lord. And, as they say, "Man up."'[63]

In other countries, religion is seen by both men and women as a way of returning to the old certainties about gender roles, but couching this in the language of rights:[64]

- 'We respect women. These new foreign ideas are confusing our women. The Bible states clearly that the woman is the priest in the home while the man is the priest in the Church. We honour them for the work they do in the home.' Paul, church leader in Uganda
- 'The church is even more resistant to change than African cultural values. For example the pope, bishops and priests are the ones who perpetuate the myth that men are superior to women from the way they treat sisters.' Paul, Zambia

- 'We believe in The Koran. The Koran says if men are 75 per cent, then women are 25 per cent ... women are less than men. If they are equal, how come the woman leaves her home to live in the husband's home?' Halima, the Gambia
- 'The Bible says women should be obedient to their husbands ... it is written that the woman was created from the rib of the man. This means the woman is inferior to the man.' Sarah, Uganda

As well as repeating the idea that men are in charge of the family, religious fundamentalists aim to move from the notion of rights to the idea that women need 'protection'. The fact that this protection is by men from other men is rarely articulated. According to women's rights activists:

religious fundamentalists often regard formal protections for women as a threat to the status of men. For example, when a Zimbabwean member of parliament opposed legislation that sought to criminalize domestic violence, he argued: 'I stand here representing God the Almighty. Women are not equal to men. This is a dangerous bill, and let it be known in Zimbabwe that the rights, privileges, and status of men are gone.'[65]

The same research also showed how fundamentalisms successfully seek to diminish women's participation in public life.

For example, in the Russian Federation, the Orthodox Church has revived stereotypes regarding women's 'natural role', pushing women back into the domestic sphere. In Southeast Asia, fundamentalist interpretations of Buddhism teach boys to be leaders and girls to be servants. From Southern Baptists in the United States to militant Muslim groups in Pakistan, and in Eritrea, France, Malaysia and Serbia, religious fundamentalists seek to limit young women's access to education.

And where conflict has led to new constitutions that are religious-based, it is often at the expense of women's rights. For example, before the 2003 invasion Iraq had one of the best records on women's rights in the region. Since 1958, under the Personal Status Law, Iraqi women have enjoyed many of the same rights as Western women. But after the invasion, the new government replaced the law with Article 2 of the new Constitution, which makes Islam the official religion and basis of legislation and leaves the interpretation of women's rights in the hands of the religious leaders.

As Houzan Mohamoud, co-founder of the Organization of Women's Freedom in Iraq, noted in an interview:

> The very first steps of this so-called democracy were Islamic Sharia law and a Shiite–Sunni divide in Iraqi society. Having an ethno-sectarian, tribalist and religious government in Iraq will only double the suffering of women, causing them to be treated as second class citizens in society. Most policies so far have been anti-women; take the recent directive of the so called women's minister whereby she wanted to impose 'modest' clothing on women employees as another step of Islamisation of Iraq.[66]

There has been considerable resistance from women, however, to the framing of religion in a way that is inimical to gender equality. For example, Sisters in Islam, from Malaysia, who regularly campaign on behalf of women's rights and for changes in misogynistic laws.[67] Malaysian artist Yati says: 'Islam gives women a very high position and a lot of rights, but over the years the patriarchal system and political power have marginalised women and made them invisible – it's a gross misunderstanding which has to be corrected. Women should reclaim their rights given by Islam.'[68]

Women's lobbying has helped to change Morocco's *Mouda-wana* (religious personal statute laws); in Turkey scholars are questioning the misogynist aspects of the Hadith (sayings and deeds attributed to the Prophet); in Indonesia's rural areas teaching materials are being revised.[69]

'We as Muslim women need to be more visible in the public arena so that people can see that we are independent beings who have a mind of their own. For too long Muslim women have been portrayed as submissive and meek. It's about time that we stand up tall and tell the world that we exist,' writes Asya Jalil, from Toronto, Canada.[70]

This is particularly important at a time when the Arab Spring has seen a backward step for women's rights as new governments are put into place to replace the old dictatorships. In Egypt, the constitution that was finalized in December 2012 was one of the reasons why many people supported the army's ousting of Mohammed Mursi's government. Omneya Talaat, a women's rights activist, said, 'We would have been doomed. The Brotherhood wanted to go back 100 years in women's rights, it was a catastrophe.'[71]

While women in Egypt were initially very much part of the demonstrations for change, soon there were stories of women being harassed, and even surrounded and raped, while they demonstrated. In these contexts, it is vital that women are supported by men.

Which is why it is vital to work with traditional and religious leaders, who are all men, to challenge some of the stereotyped ways in which women are viewed. And though they may not be heard as much as some of the more radical anti-feminist voices, such men do exist. For example, Amir Rashidi, a man who is part of the Iranian women's rights and democratic movement and an active member of the 'One Million Signature Campaign against Discriminating Laws', says:

> Today the women's rights activists are still very active in Iran. They organize workshops and seminars, but it became much more difficult than before. The pressure from the government has increased severely, and even lawyers are arrested. It became more difficult and has slowed down, but our work

---

Men stand up for women in Cairo[72]

A roped-off section of staircase creates a safe passage for women as they exit the metro in Cairo's Tahrir Square during protests.

But it is not manned by transport security, or the police. It is male volunteers who cordon off a pathway so that women can get into the square without being pressed upon by the men already outside.

These volunteers are protecting women against minor incidents of sexual harassment: touching and groping. But brutal attacks continue to take place.

Hassan Nassar, a 22-year-old youth activist, spent much of last week's protests working to protect women in Tahrir Square. He spent some time bringing women out of the metro, and other times patrolling the area.

Women who have been victims of assault, and witnesses too, report a similar sequence of events. They say

has not stopped. I believe that this movement cannot be stopped as long as there is at least one person who believes in equality.[73]

Across the world in Indonesia, the MenCare+ programme, run by Dutch non-governmental organization Rutgers WFP and Instituto Promundo,[74] found another example of a religious man prepared to make the changes in his own life that then became an example to others. When Muhammad Nur Salim, a Muslim preacher, first started sharing domestic chores and the care of their two small children with his wife, a head teacher, the other

a group of men isolates the woman, then other men on the outside tell onlookers they are trying to help someone in distress.

'We go into the middle of crowds to get the girls out and take them to a car to get away,' Mr Nassar says. 'I do it because this doesn't belong in our society. You can imagine it's your sister or your mum and you have to help.'

Sexual assaults during protests in Tahrir Square, in particular since the mass protests against a power-grabbing constitutional declaration in November 2012, have become so frequent that activist groups have formed to take action against them.

One of the groups is Operation Anti-Sexual Harassment and Assault. Their volunteers alone helped more than 150 women following incidents of physical sexual harassment, including three rapes, between 30 June and 3 July 2013.

villages thought they were strange, especially in such a traditional area of East Java, where patriarchal values still hold strong. Nur Salim's story has been made into a short film by prominent Indonesian film-maker Nia Dinata, who saw the way in which the villagers started to emulate their leader, and started to show more empathy with their wives. Nia Dinata told the *Jakarta Post*: 'I saw with my own eyes that this preacher practiced what he preached – a very loving and caring husband and father. He has led his villagers into being individuals who really care for their family members.'[75]

Changing generations, changing attitudes

Young people I have met in many countries, including most recently in Indonesia, say they are more educated than their parents, and they are exposed to a wider range of ideas through the Internet or television. As a result, many are challenging their parents' deeply held beliefs about what it means to be a man or a woman, a girl or a boy.

This mother from Fiji notes: 'Men in the past were very strict about tradition and that everything they do be done the traditional way. ... Nowadays, parents – including fathers – let their daughters have more freedom, [for example] if they want to dress a certain way. ... Because life in general is changing, it's hard to keep the traditional way of raising children.'[76]

A six-country study also found that younger men, and those with more education, had more gender-equitable views than their parents.[77] A World Bank report notes: 'The willingness of mothers and fathers to embrace gender equality in their children's education may bring massive change and make gender relations in the next generation more equitable and harmonious.'[78]

In the same study,[79] in Bhutan mothers' aspirations for their sons include a more direct reference to gender equality: 'Equality for both would make the biggest difference in the lives of our daughters and would imbue our sons with the understanding that all humans of opposite gender are same.' These women said they 'would love to see their girl and boy children take equal stand in all sectors, where girls will not be the underprivileged gender'.

The report notes that: 'Just as with their daughters, mothers socialize their sons and can also be key agents for change in their sons' attitudes and behaviors,' recognizing, along with masculinities expert Michael Kaufman, that both women and men can hand down traditional notions of what it is to be a man or a woman and that this can be either liberating or restrictive. Kaufman says: 'gender roles are constructed and reconstructed – and must be questioned – by both men and women. Girls and women can contribute to traditional harmful versions of manhood, just as boys and men can contribute to traditional, restrictive versions of womanhood.'[80]

There are increasing numbers of women – and men – who are challenging these stereotypes. For example, in the UK, a project called 'Great men value women' encourages male volunteers aged eighteen to twenty-eight to talk to younger boys in schools. Its website[81] says: 'Great Men was born out of the reasoning that men have a key role to play in the struggle for gender equality and that men and women's liberation are tied together.'

Rapper, comedian and writer Doc Brown explained that he was:

an accidental feminist; I was raised by women and it was something I began thinking about before I analysed the importance of it in my own head. ... Girls are people, they got the same needs and requirements as you but what is really scary is that men older than us have created a world in which we are supposed to believe that these girls are somehow secondary to us. You have got to get the word out when they are young – because once they hit year 9 [age thirteen to fourteen] that is when they start to think that females are just objects.[82]

In Ecuador,[83] a network of young people – originally all men – call themselves Cascos Rosa, or 'Pink Helmets' – 'We seek and promote gender equality and equal rights and opportunities for men and women,' said Damián Valencia, one of the thirty-three founders. The pink helmets and T-shirts 'break the stereotype that only women wear pink; that boy babies are dressed in blue and girls in pink', he added.

The group was started in 2010 by teenagers and young adults who had been trained by the Ecuadorean chapter of Acción Ciudadana por la Democracia y el Desarrollo (ACDemocracia – Citizens' Action for Democracy and Development) and the Coalition against Trafficking in Women and Girls in Latin America and the Caribbean.

Valencia said that gender equity 'is such a huge problem that it affects everyone'. He acknowledged that 'an improvement can be seen' in the country, but added that 'even so, we are still living in a patriarchal society'.

Belonging to Cascos Rosa has had a major impact on his life, he said. At home there was 'a *machista* scheme of things' in which the men 'did not wash clothes or do the ironing, did not cook or wash dishes, and expected everything to be done for them.

'Now we all share the same jobs at home, no one is above anyone else, and we have the same rights and opportunities,' he went on.

Carolina Félix, who runs workshops for the network, says, 'A definite change is taking place.' She believes the new generation 'are not afraid of showing themselves as they are, and neither do they say, "poor women, such victims!" because it is an issue both men and women have to work on'.

This chapter has looked at how the attitudes towards being male or female are shaped at an early age. It has examined the many forces that continue to harden those attitudes into particular kinds of beliefs and behaviours as young people grow up – in particular religious conservatism, consumerism and pornography. It has shown how attitudes are changed – and where they are not. And it has linked these changes to the wider debates about what it means to be a man or a woman and how this feeds into a feminist discourse and promotes – or hinders – equality between the genders.

The next chapter looks at what can be done to bring a gender equality focus for both men and women to health and education.

4 | NO ZERO-SUM GAME: EDUCATION AND HEALTH

A free human being

If anyone stands as a symbol for the importance of education, and in particular girls' education, it is seventeen-year-old Malala Yousafzai, who was shot by the Taliban in Pakistan for promoting the right of girls to go to school. In an interview on BBC radio, she talked about the importance of her father's support:

> My father believes in equality and he said that girls and boys have the same equal rights. And he accepted me as his daughter but also as a free human being and he gave me freedom and accepted me as he accepted my brothers. He said: 'I want the same education for my daughter as my sons are getting'. This is really an important thing for girls in our society because it is hard for them to get an education.[1]

The benefits of education for girls – and for gender equality – are clear. First, for the girls themselves in terms of knowledge, skills, self-confidence and socialization. And secondly, for the women they will become. Educated women have lower fertility, their children have better health and nutrition – and they are more likely to go to school.[2] The United Nations Population Fund says: 'Girls who have been educated are likely to marry later and to have smaller and healthier families. Educated women can recognize the importance of health care and know how to seek it for themselves and their children. Education helps girls and women to know their rights and to gain confidence to claim them.'[3] Confidence that Malala so obviously has, at least in part thanks to her father's support.

But this focus on girls' education may have masked another trend – and that is that boys in many countries are increasingly dropping out of school. In Latin America and the Caribbean and in much of the so-called 'rich world', girls are doing better than boys at school, and staying on longer. In the Dominican Republic, for example, only 64 per cent of boys stay on until the last grade of primary school compared with 74 per cent of girls.[4] In the UK, in 2010, the pass rate for girls taking examinations at age sixteen was 72.6 per cent, compared with 65.4 per cent for boys.[5]

This is likely to have consequences for both sexes, because education is good for boys too and for the women they live with – for example, a multi-country study in 2010 found that men who completed secondary education held more gender-equitable attitudes, were more likely to be there for their child's birth and involved in childcare and less likely to be violent towards women.[6]

With regard to women's health, there is a similar story, although there is still a long way to go before girls and women receive the healthcare that they are entitled to. At least one woman still dies every minute from complications related to pregnancy or childbirth – that adds up to 287,000 women a year. In addition, around ten million more women suffer injury, infection or disease as a result of giving birth.[7] And 50 per cent of women still do not get the healthcare they need.[8]

But there also needs to be a focus on men's health – for example, men in almost every country have a lower life expectancy than women. And yet the United Nations' Gender Inequality Index on health has indicators only for women.[9] There is no equivalent index for men. A study in the British medical journal *The Lancet* notes: 'Global health policies and programmes focused on prevention of and care for the health needs of men are notably absent.'[10]

The emphasis on women and girls has meant that boys' education and men's health have either been ignored, or are not part of gender policies and practices, or perhaps have been debated in different fora.

The result is that, once again, the discussions on health and education for men and boys and women and girls have often run on parallel tracks so that no one is looking at the perspective from both sides.

But it is hard, even in a chapter like this, to avoid being binary. But this is not a zero-sum game. In order to achieve the best for both sexes, the approach to both education and health needs to be holistic. And it needs to keep the focus firmly on gender equality using a feminist lens.

For this to happen, the crucial question is this: how to keep the perspective on education and health for women and girls, which remains crucial because of their multiple disadvantages, but combine it with an equal emphasis on the problems for boys and men – which also has a positive effect on the women in their lives?

The two things are not in opposition, though there may be competition for resources. Improving the education and the health of both sexes is something that should concern feminists and those working for women's rights as well as men who want to see a more gender-equal future.

This chapter looks at what prevents girls and boys from going to school. It looks at parents' aspirations for their sons and daughters. It looks at the consequences of the neglect of men's health. Finally, it outlines the ever-shifting challenges that remain, and examines the consequences for girls and women, and boys and men, and for gender equality, if these are not addressed.

Standing on their own feet: why girls don't go to school

There are many reasons why girls in so many countries do not go to school – because their parents won't let them, because there are no schools or they are far away, because they have to stay at home to look after younger children, because they are married very young, because they have to work. But perhaps this story from my visit to Pakistan in 2012[11] is a more effective way of explaining what the problems are.

In Pakistan's remote and rural areas, only 60 per cent of primary-school-age children attend school. There are only 56 girls for every 100 boys.[12] This is partly because there are more boys' schools than girls' – for example, in Thatta district, in Sindh, there are 2,700 schools for boys and only 330 for girls. It is also because parents value boys' education more than girls'.

As a result, overall literacy is very low in Pakistan, at 55.5 per cent,[13] and the difference between urban and rural and women and men is stark. If you are a boy living in a city, you have an 80 per cent chance of going to school. If you are a girl in a village, it drops to 34 per cent. In some rural districts, only one in ten women is literate, compared with half the men.

In the rural areas that I visited in 2012, I found very few girls who attended school. Rabia Bibi, aged ten, was one. Her village is a long way from anywhere. There is no government school, even a primary one, close by. Only 7 per cent of villages in Pakistan have government schools that are only one or two kilometres away, and 26 per cent have schools between three and five kilometres or more away.[14] With bad roads and little transport, the only option for most is to walk. Poor parents cannot spare the time to accompany their children, so most, like the girls in Rabia's village, stay at home instead.

Savera, a bright-eyed ten-year-old in shocking pink, is one of a handful of girls in her village who attends a boys' school because there is none for the girls. 'It is written outside the school that it is a boys' middle school, but some of us girls do go,' she says. 'We go together, but when we get older the men will stop us going because there is no man to go with us and keep us safe.'

Rabia goes to a private school, a privilege that she is granted only because she is the daughter of the village president. But she would much rather be with her friends. She has tried to persuade them to attend, but, she says: 'Their fathers are not convinced that it is worth sending a girl to school.' And besides that, she says, shrugging resignedly, 'they can't afford it'. If parents have money to send a child to school, it will still almost always be a son rather than a daughter.

Rabia's father has enough resources to send her brothers and sisters to school as well, but many of the other girls in the village cannot read and write, though some say they have learned to read the Qur'an. Aziza, aged fifteen, has to get someone else to write even her name. 'I would like to go to school,' she says, 'but none is available close by.'

Farzana, aged fourteen, who looks younger than her years, says she did go to school until Grade 3: 'But I am grown up now. I cannot go to school any more. I make clothes, do embroidery; I give the money to my mother.' Savera too says that she already has chores to do at home – sweeping floors, washing dishes, taking care of younger children – and these will increase as she grows up, leaving her little time for studying. Zeinab, aged twelve, points out one of the other main reasons why girls do not go to school, and it is not because they do not want to: 'I want to go to school, but my father will not allow it.'

Boys just want to play?

For boys, the story is a very different one. And at least part of this story is directly related to how society sees masculinities – and so to the story of men's involvement in gender equality and feminism. In an increasing number of countries, boys are either dropping out of school or doing worse academically than their sisters. Barry Chevannes, Professor of Social Anthropology at the University of the West Indies, said that: 'There is no doubt in my mind that male alienation from the school system contributes to all the social problems that we have come across.' He believes that if boys were educated, there would be a reduction in violence, irresponsible sexual behaviour and other risky behaviours.[15]

Take Juan, aged seventeen, from the Dominican Republic, whom I interviewed in 2010. His older sisters are in college; his mother Ramona, aged fifty, has gone back to studying because she wants to be a nurse. Juan tells me: 'There are a lot more girls than boys in my school. Some of my [male] friends are already working, others don't like to study. But I like studying and I would like to do something in music when I finish school.'[16]

In the UK, a study by the Joseph Rowntree Foundation of young men's attitudes to gender and work noted that: 'Notions of masculinity appeared to play a significant part in the majority of these young men's poor use of school. Having a laugh, resisting teachers' influence, acting tough and the displacement of emotions away from appearing weak and vulnerable were recurrent themes.'[17] Most of the young men interviewed later said they regretted dropping out.

So why are boys not in school in some countries, notably Latin America and the Caribbean and the 'rich' world, while their sisters remain at their desks? And what does this mean for them, and for the rest of society?

Sometimes, it is simply due to poverty. Studies of child labour have found that boys are more likely to leave school in order to work for money than girls, although a major reason for girls dropping out is related to domestic work in the home.[18] For example, a World Bank study in Vietnam found that 'in the poorest households girls are especially more likely to enroll than boys (perhaps because of work demands for boys)'.[19] Class, race and poverty are all contributing factors, as are urban/rural divides.

But often there is a link to the way that boys are socialized to be male. For example, there is increasing evidence that in a number of countries, boys are becoming disaffected with school and that has to do with the way that schools organize learning. Most teachers are female. And some educationists believe that the curriculum has become increasingly 'feminized' with an emphasis on sitting quietly at desks rather than more active ways of learning that might suit boys better.[20] 'Part of why girls are really kicking boys' butts is it's become feminine to be smart, or it's become feminine to have a strong work ethic. And to counter, it's become masculine to be a bum or to be lazy or to not appreciate work,' says B. Lesley Cumberbatch, of CW Jefferys Collegiate Institute, Canada.[21] Asking for help, even succeeding at school, has somehow become something girls do – so boys would prefer to be seen as 'cool' by their peers, which means not studying, acting up and even failing their exams.

In Latin America and the Caribbean, the United Nations Girls' Education Initiative (UNGEI) noted: 'The region has substantial work ahead to make school, especially at the secondary

	Maths			Vietnamese		
	First test	Second test	Gain	First test	Second test	Gain
Girls	503.05	540.69	37.64	514.57	528.16	13.59
Boys	497.33	539.38	42.05	487.54	500.95	13.41
Difference	5.72	1.31	4.41	27.03	27.21	0.18

2 Learning achievement and progress, by gender, Vietnam[22]

level, attractive and welcoming to boys and young men.'[23] 'The boys just want to play, the girls don't, they're interested when the teacher tells about the homework. I think this is why girls achieve more than boys,' says Thais, aged eleven, from Brazil.[24] In Vietnam, a paper from Oxford University's Young Lives study[25] found that girls had higher academic confidence and academic effort scores than boys, and these resulted in higher academic scores, although boys caught up somewhat in maths by the second test. The difference between the sexes was up to a year's average learning. These results were similar to another study in Vietnam undertaken by the World Bank.[26]

Teachers too may have their own gender biases and therefore have different expectations of boys and girls. There may be very little about gender attitudes in teacher training curricula that helps teachers to be more aware of their own preconceived ideas.[27] Boys have few role models in school, because in many countries schools are populated by female teachers. The only men are often at the top, with much less interaction with the children and young people. In England, for example, in 2010 there were no male trainee nursery teachers.[28] In Brazil, only one in 1,000 daycare workers are men.[29]

The 'Men Who Care'[30] qualitative study in five countries (Brazil, Chile, India, Mexico and South Africa) found that men who wanted to work in schools or daycare faced prejudice from parents and from their peers, as this twenty-two-year-old daycare provider pointed out: 'Because when you work in a daycare, people don't think of the pedagogical work you're doing. They think you're changing diapers. So they [my friends] think it's funny that I have an inclination towards that ...' This male nurse in India said: 'Male nurses feel a little uncomfortable. The nursing profession is 90 per cent women. It is a little difficult for men to adjust [to] it.'

In addition, male teachers are more likely to have difficulty with people being suspicious about their motives for working with children. This teacher in Mexico said: 'I was afraid because in the school where I taught there were professors who were given a hard time because they had touched the girls in the primary and secondary classes they taught, but they didn't do it maliciously (it was misunderstood).'

Another theory about why boys do worse than girls in school is that boys in richer countries spend so much time interacting with technology that they have little time for study. This becomes particularly acute once they become adolescents, says an American study by the Henry J. Kaiser Family Foundation. Although both sexes continue to use computers for a range of activities, including social networking, among fifteen- to eighteen-year-olds girls have lost interest in computer games. The report notes: 'Girls go from an average of 12 minutes a day playing computer games when they are in the 8- to 10-year-old group, down to just three minutes a day by the time they are 15 to 18 years old; there is no such decrease among boys.'[31] While the link between technology use and failure at school is not definitive, studies do seem to show that boys who play video games a lot may spend less time doing other things. One study by an assistant professor at Denison University in Granville, Ohio, found that boys aged six to nine who owned a video-gaming system at home 'spent less time doing homework, reading for fun or being read to by their parents. After barely five months, their scores on reading and writing assessments were significantly lower than those of the boys who didn't own a console.'[32]

The factors of race and class come in here too, in that it is mostly boys from low-income or marginalized families and communities who have real problems in school. For example, in both the USA and Brazil, young people of African descent are less likely to be in school than their peers. And for these boys, in fact, education may not be the best route into earning a living. Research in Brazil has found, for example, that for a boy from a favela in Rio de Janeiro, secondary education does not lead to paid work in the same way it does for boys from more prosperous areas.[33] This is not only because they are disadvantaged by racism and classism but also because school does not teach them to understand how to operate in the formal workplace. The same is true in much of the Caribbean, as this young man from Kingston, Jamaica, said: 'You can pass secondary with five subjects and still not find a good job.'[34]

High levels of dropout by boys and young men can have serious consequences not only for the boys themselves, but for girls, and for society as a whole. In Latin America and the Caribbean, the United Nations Girls' Education Initiative (UNGEI) said: 'The consequences of illiteracy and under-education for boys and men have dire consequences for society. ... This has been particularly problematic in Jamaica, where domestic abuse, gang lawlessness and crime are on the rise.'[35] Jamaica has one of the highest homicide rates in the world. It also has a culture that holds strong stereotypes about masculinities, which are reinforced rather than countered in school. According to the World Bank, 30 per cent of boys in Grade 6 were reading below their grade level.[36] Which is why programmes like 'Change from Within' are key. It aims to improve boys' achievement by moving beyond a focus on academic performance. A review found that it had succeeded in reducing school violence 'by identifying and building on positive features in schools, and by changing a culture of dependency on external interventions to one of self-reliance'.[37]

Parivartan: using sport to change boys' attitudes[38]

Most boys and young men are interested in sport. The Parivartan programme in India uses cricket to work on gender equality. It is modelled on the US-based Coaching Boys into Men programme at Futures Without Violence (formerly Family Violence Fund).

Parivartan, which means 'change for the better', aims to help boys and young men aged ten to sixteen to see women and girls as equals, and treat them with respect, and in doing so reduce gender-based violence. In discussions, it challenges the boys to question traditional notions about manhood and men's and women's roles in society.

Launched in March 2010, the programme enlists cricket players, coaches and community mentors to serve as positive role models for school-age boys in more than one hundred Mumbai schools. It teaches that aggressive, violent behaviour doesn't make them 'real men' – nor does it help win cricket matches.

Leena Joshi, director of Apnalaya, one of the main local partners in the Parivartan programme, told Gillian Gaynair from the International Center for Research on Women (ICRW) that she believes the effort is timely – if not overdue. 'We have all worked – NGOs, governments – on women's issues very specifically,' Joshi says, 'and I think in the whole process, the men have been left behind.'

An evaluation of the programme after three years showed that participants were less tolerant of abuse against women, and that their perceptions about what it means to be a man also shifted. Zaheer, one of the participants, said: 'I started questioning my identity, my attitude, the way I behave and treat myself, my family, neighbors and especially girls and women in my locality and elsewhere.'[39]

'I've learned how to be polite, how to talk, how to be respectful to girls and women,' said Jadhav.

'I've learned that controlling is not a way to love a girl, but [the way to love] is to give her space in her life,' said Parivartan mentor twenty-year-old Rajesh Jadha.

The programme has also had positive effects on boys' education. For example, Zaheer, who was regularly skipping school, is now back in twelfth grade. He also has a job with a non-profit organization that works on social issues. And he is training to be a cricket coach.

'I have an ambition in life,' he said. 'Now when I look back, I realize the difference [in my life], and I think that's what is my turning point.'[40]

Wearing a white toga: parents' aspirations

Mothers and fathers in many countries increasingly seem to have similar aspirations for their sons and daughters. They want their children's lives, both girls' and boys', to be better than their own – though sometimes, faced with the dilemma of not being able to afford to send both to school, they still choose the boy in the hope that he will be the one to financially support them in their old age.

As part of their 'Because I am a girl' campaign and report, Plan International is following 135 girls in nine countries who were born in 2006. Parents and caregivers were interviewed in 2010 about their aspirations for their small daughters:

Mary Joy's mother in the Philippines said: 'Being the only parent left, I want Mary Joy to finish her studies. How I wish seeing her wearing a white toga at her high school graduation. She will study here in our village for elementary, and hopefully move to our relatives in Catarman for her secondary education. She will be taken care of there. Hopefully God will guide me in fulfilling my dreams for my child Mary Joy.'[41]

Charnel's father in Benin believed: 'It would not advantage us to keep our daughter out of school. A girl who goes to school will succeed in life and can take over from us in the future.'

A number of women hope that their daughters' education will help them to achieve more in life than their mothers did. Consolata's mother in Benin says: 'They say that by educating a girl, you educate a nation. I agree; if I had had more schooling I would be a professional today. I hope that my daughter is able to complete her education in my place in order to overcome this challenge.' In the Dominican Republic, Noelia's grandmother, who is bringing her up while her mother works in the city, said: 'Of course [it is important for a girl to be educated]. That's

The Gender Equity Movement in Schools (GEMS) in India[42]

Recognizing that attitudes towards gender are formed at an early age, the Gender Equity Movement in Schools (GEMS) programme aims to foster gender equity, improve sexual and reproductive health and reduce violence among boys and girls aged twelve to eighteen and their teachers in India. It is being implemented by ICRW, Instituto Promundo and in partnership with the Committee of Resource Organizations for Literacy (CORO) and the Tata Institute for Social Sciences (TISS), in collaboration with municipalities and public schools in Mumbai, Goa and the Kota district of Rajasthan. The project is also testing work with fathers of daughters.

An evaluation of the project in Mumbai with 1,100 students found that the percentage of girls who held more gender-equitable attitudes increased from 23 to 53 per cent of girls and from 24 to 39 per cent of boys. One of the challenges was to find safe spaces for such discussions, as one report notes: 'For this reason, it is important to think about ways that programmes can continue to offer activities for single-sex groups while also providing opportunities for mixed-sex groups to come together, learn from each other, and make shared commitments to social change.'[43]

Following the success of the pilot phase in Mumbai, the Maharashtra state government has integrated key elements of GEMS in the school gender programme for all of its nearly 25,000 public schools, and the idea is also being rolled out in Vietnam.

the best way to live. I don't want her to have a life as tough as mine.'

Soumeyatou's father in Togo said: 'The education of the girl-child is of equal importance because she could eventually be able to take care of herself and no one can cheat her. She could work to support her family.'

Chea's mother in Cambodia, however, said that if she had to choose which child to send to higher education, she would

	Disagree	Agree
India	32	63
Pakistan	39	51
Egypt	47	50
China	50	48
Jordan	54	44
Japan	64	35
Poland	58	34
Nigeria	66	34
Indonesia	71	28
South Korea	69	27
Turkey	69	25
Russia	73	22
Kenya	77	22
Germany	83	16
USA	83	15
Mexico	84	14
France	87	14
Brazil	87	11
Argentina	88	10
Britain	97	9
Spain	93	7
Lebanon	97	4

3 A university education is more important for a boy than for a girl (%)[44]

choose her son. If she had the resources, however, she would like both children to go.

Some parents may even have higher expectations of their daughters than of their sons – one survey in Canada found that 'parents of 15 year-old girls are more likely to expect their daughter to complete a university degree than parents of boys of the same age, and that boys are less likely to report that all their friends intend to go to university'.[45]

Opinion on whether girls' education or boys' education is more important still seems to be divided, as a recent poll by the Pew Research Center shows.[46] Asked to agree or disagree with the statement 'A university education is more important for a boy than for a girl', more than six out of ten people in India agreed. In Pakistan (51 per cent), Egypt (50 per cent) and China (48 per cent), about half the respondents also agreed, while in Britain, Brazil, France, Mexico and Germany more than 80 per cent disagreed, and almost all in Lebanon (97 per cent).

We have seen in this section that girls' education has rightly become an important focus of international attention. I have looked briefly at why so many girls don't go to school and at what can encourage them to go, but also at the factors that are now preventing so many boys and young men from getting an education – at a cost not only to themselves, but to women and girls and society as a whole. The next section looks at health, where there are similarly parallel discourses of disadvantage that are being dealt with separately rather than being seen as part of a whole.

'Real men don't get sick'?

When it comes to health, a strong focus on girls' and women's health continues to be key. But there also seems to be a neglect of men's health. For example, the United Nations' *Human De-velopment Reports*[47] have a Gender Inequality Index on health which only has indicators for women. Its rationale, as stated on the website, is:

> reproductive health indicators used in the Gender Inequality Index do not have equivalent indicators for men. So in this dimension, the reproductive health of girls and women is compared to what should be societal goals – no maternal death, and no adolescent pregnancy. The rationale is that safe motherhood reflects the importance society attaches to women's reproductive role. Early childbearing, as measured by the adolescent fertility rate, is associated with greater health risks for mothers and infants; also, adolescent mothers often are forced out of school and into low-skilled jobs.[48]

This is fine; the problem is that there is no equivalent index for men.

A study published in the British medical journal *The Lancet*[49] of international development organizations' gender policies found that while gender is meant to be about both women and men and the relationships between them, very often gender means 'addressing gender inequalities and strengthening the response for women and girls (Global Fund to Fight AIDS, TB, and Malaria), focusing on women and girls (United States Agency for International Development [USAID], United States Global Health Initiative, UNDP, UK Department for International Development [DfID]), or normalizing existing health and survival inequalities – the World Economic Forum calculates a global gender gap index on the basis that women live five years longer than men'.

The upshot of all this is that, in fact, men die younger than

women. Although life expectancy is improving in most countries, it is improving more slowly for men than for women. The
same study noted that: 'decreases in mortality were smaller in
men than in females of all age groups. The smallest decrease in
mortality rates during 1970–2010 was in young men aged 25–39
years, possibly because of injuries – globally, road injuries kill
three times more men than women'.[50] It also noted that: 'the top
ten contributors to global disability-adjusted life-years (DALY)
have greater burdens on men than on women'.[51]

The reasons generally given for why men die younger than
women tend to blame men for not taking better care of their
health, for indulging in excessive alcohol and drug consumption,
dangerous driving and unsafe sex – and for not seeking medical
help until it is too late.

And it is true that young men in particular are less likely
than young women to consult a doctor if they are sick, and
more likely to indulge in risky behaviours. Most of this is linked
to traditional views of what it means and what it takes to be a
man. For example, one survey in the USA of young men aged
fifteen to nineteen found that those who held traditional views of
manhood were more likely to report substance use, violence and
delinquency and unsafe sexual practices.[52] As one Zimbabwean
man put it, 'real men don't get sick'.[53]

These behaviours are harmful to women, and they are also
very damaging for young men themselves. All over the world,
men aged fifteen to twenty-four have among the highest rates
of death by traffic accidents, suicide and violence, all of which
are related to the way that they are socialized to be men.[54] In
Jamaica, Brazil, Colombia and some countries in sub-Saharan
Africa, higher numbers of young men die in these ways than
in conflicts elsewhere. Even in western Europe, these external

causes make up more than 60 per cent of mortalities among boys and young men from birth to age twenty-four.[55]

In the UK, suicide accounted for the deaths of more young men in England and Wales in 2011 than road death, murder and HIV/AIDs combined.[56] In 2012, the Office for National Statistics reported that there were 4,590 male suicides compared to 1,391 female suicides, the equivalent of 18.2 per 100,000 men and 5.2 per 100,000 women. This means that men are three times more likely to kill themselves than women – the highest ratio for more than thirty years. In an interview with the *Guardian* newspaper, Clare Wylie, head of policy and research at the counselling service the Samaritans, said: 'Society has this masculine ideal that people are expecting to live up to. Lots of that has to do with being a breadwinner. When men don't live up to that it can be quite devastating for them.' Paul Bristow, from the Mental Health Foundation, said: 'We urgently need to know more about why being male is itself a risk factor in suicide and to do more to help men, especially young men, seek assistance rather than suffer in silence.'[57]

	Women	Men
Norway	6.5	17.3
Australia	3.6	12.8
United States	4.5	17.7
Netherlands	5.5	13.1
Germany	6	17.9
New Zealand	5.5	18.1
Ireland	4.7	19
Sweden	6.8	18.7
Switzerland	11.4	24.8
Japan	13.2	36.2

4 Suicides, women and men, per 100,000 people, 2001–10[58]

There are no statistics on this for the poorest countries in the world, but for the rich world overall, 6.6 women out of 100,000 take their own lives compared with 20.6 men – more than three times as many. In most countries where statistics are available, double the number of men commit suicide compared to women.

In fact, equal numbers of women and men say they contemplate suicide, but more than twice the number of men make successful attempts. Jane Powell, coordinator of the Campaign Against Living Miserably (CALM), says:

> it's a very tricky thought that young men might need care
> and attention, because they are very often seen as the cause
> of the problems. The one thing that they are supposed to
> still be is strong and silent, and if you are going to be silent,
> then of course you are not going to take any action over the
> problems that face you, and if that's the case it's just going to
> get worse.[59]

Many young men are engaged in a range of risky behaviours. In some countries, young men between fifteen and twenty-four believe that 'real men' don't use contraceptives – while in the rich world and parts of Latin America and the Caribbean rates are between 63 and 93 per cent; in most sub-Saharan African countries, fewer than 50 per cent of young men practise safe sex.[60] One study in the USA found that 'more than four out of five male 7th- to 12th-grade students engaging in unprotected intercourse also participate regularly in one or more additional health risk behaviors. One in five young men report having been drunk or on a drug high the last time they had intercourse.'[61]

High-risk sex has terrible consequences when it comes to HIV and AIDS. At the end of 2010, there were 34 million people living with HIV, half of whom were men and half women, although

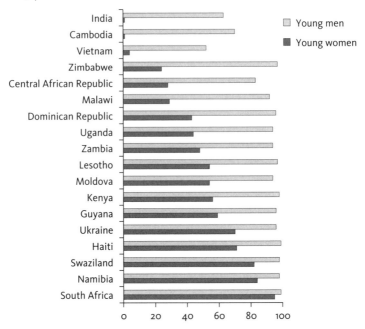

5 Percentage of young people aged fifteen to nineteen who had higher-risk sex with a non-marital, non-cohabitating partner in the last year, selected countries[62]

this ratio varies from country to country and region to region.[63] Over 50 per cent of those newly infected are between fifteen and twenty-four years old. And once again, studies show that men with more traditional views of masculinity and who believe that men are superior to women 'are more likely to practice unsafe sex, treat women violently and abuse substances – thus placing themselves, their partners, and their families at risk of HIV'.[64] The International HIV/AIDS Alliance notes that: 'Prescribed masculine traits, such as the notion that men's sexual needs are uncontrollable or that men should have multiple sexual partners, also have serious consequences for men's health, placing them – and thus their partners – at high risk of HIV infection.'[65]

Not surprisingly perhaps, men are therefore reluctant to be tested, which means that they are not on treatment and are likely to infect any sexual partners, and eventually to die. In his book *Sizwe's Test: A Young Man's Journey through Africa's AIDS Epidemic*, South African journalist Jonny Steinberg remembers his first meeting with Sizwe: "'I have not tested", he said. "My girlfriend is pregnant and she went to the clinic to test. She's negative. Do you think that means I am definitely negative?" I was taken aback by his openness. "If you want to know, you must test," I said. "I know," he replied. "But I'm scared."'[66] 'Going to the clinic is regarded as a sign of weakness, of being "not man enough",' says Patrick Godana, of South African NGO Sonke Gender Justice.[67]

In many developing countries, many more women than men are now accessing ART (anti-retroviral treatment). For example, in South Africa, in 2011, 60 per cent of women who were eligible were being treated compared with 41 per cent of men,[68] and men are at a more advanced stage of the disease when they start treatment.[69]

'The hope for winning the fight with the HIV/AIDS pandemic lies in changing the attitudes and behaviour of the boys of today, the men of tomorrow, who will not be afraid of equality with women and who are willing to change their behaviour and attitudes,' says Njoki Wainaina, a gender activist in Kenya.[70]

Working together for gender equality

There is, understandably, anxiety on the part of those working with girls and women that working with men and boys on this issue will take both the focus and the money away from women's health or education. One study[71] sounds a note of caution: 'Achievement of equitable health outcomes for women and men should not involve diversion of resources from existing women-focused programmes – eg, reduction of maternal mortality, or addressing of violence against women. Instead, the global health community should advocate additional investments in other burdens of ill health which are equally damaging to the health of individuals and societies.' The answer is not that men's health and women's health should be pitted against each other, but that an analysis of the damaging effects of traditional masculinities would also benefit women – and promote gender equality.

There are signs that, in some places at least, men are changing, as the box below shows.

The Men's Travelling Conference: changing traditional beliefs in Africa[72]

Lynda Birungi, from the national family planning group Reproductive Health Uganda, says more young fathers are becoming involved in family planning than before largely for financial reasons. However, these men are still a minority.

'Out of every five women who come to our clinic, only one comes with a man. But over twenty years ago, no men came. These days, the young generation of male partners want a better standard of living and feel that they can attain this by having small families,' Birungi says.

Meanwhile, in Malawi, what started as a travelling theatre of only 10 police officers 11 years ago has now grown to a movement of over a thousand men preaching against gender-based violence, which fuels unwanted pregnancies and increases maternal mortality.

The group, the Men's Travelling Conference (MTC), is

a team of mostly men and some women funded by the Norwegian government and the United Nations Population Fund.

In 2003, the MTC marked the annual 16 Days of Activism Against Gender Violence, an international campaign calling for non-violence against women and children that is held from Nov. 25 to Dec. 10, in a unique way.

Men from Kenya, Zambia and Ethiopia converged on Malawi's capital Lilongwe after travelling there by bus. Along the way, the men stopped at each community they passed, and left behind the message that violence against women was destructive and that men hold the power and responsibility to stop such violence ...

'Ten years ago, my clinic in Bamako only used to receive women, but today the women are being accompanied by their husbands and that to me is a sign that what we are doing is working,' says Mountaga Toure, executive director for the Malian Association for the Protection and Promotion of the Family, known by its French acronym as AMPFF. The association is an affiliate of the International Planned Parenthood Federation (IPPF).

'I sometimes see men coming on their own to collect contraceptives for their partners, saying that their wives are too busy to do that,' he tells IPS in a telephonic interview. This, he says, is a massive change in a deeply Muslim country like Mali.

Toure says that the AMPFF, in partnership with the IPPF, is deliberately encouraging men to talk about what has always been regarded as taboo.

'To make them understand, we talk about the economy and whether it can allow any man to support 10 children ... this makes them understand the reason why they need to plan with their wives how many children their pockets can support,' Toure says.

What is needed is a focus on the different needs of girls and boys, men and women, when it comes to health or education. It sounds obvious. But in practice, work on girls' education rarely considers boys, and work on men is done in isolation from work on women, so tensions inevitably arise.

I was told of one programme in South Africa where the girls, who were the focus of the training, were gathered in a room while the boys jumped up and down outside, desperate to see in through the windows. I was in a meeting where a participant told of a reproductive health project for young people. All the staff were women, all the clients were girls. The boys did not dare seek help for fear of being laughed at by their peers. So again, they hung around outside.

Working with men and women is a win-win strategy. As one paper notes: 'Much good work has been done in gender-transformative programs with one sex or the other. But more could be accomplished by working in a synchronized manner with both. What is generally missing from every single-sex approach is the broader awareness of how gender norms are reinforced by everyone in the community.' The authors call this a 'gender-synchronized' approach.[73]

There are a growing number of programmes that work with

both women and men on health issues. Stepping Stones, for example, includes both men and women in creative work on sexual health and HIV prevention and at the same time work towards building more gender-equitable relationships. It is a testament to the need for such work that since it was established in 1995 in Uganda, the Stepping Stones manual has been implemented in over forty countries, translated into thirteen languages, and used with hundreds of thousands of individuals on all continents.[74]

ReproSalud, in Peru, is implemented by Manuela Ramos, a women's advocacy organization. It was the women who asked the organization to work with men, both to deal with men's opposition to the work they were doing and to explore with men the connections between masculinity, relationships, health and violence. ReproSalud saw the issue as 'working with men on women's terms',[75] and an evaluation of the programme found that it had positive results for both women and men.[76]

'Between Us' in Brazil: for young men and young women[77]

Entre Nós ('Between Us'), run by Instituto Promundo in Brazil, grew out of two successful programmes run for young men – Programme H ('H' for *homens/hombres* or men in Portuguese and Spanish) – and young women – Programme M (for *mulheres/mujeres* or women) that are now run in a number of other countries besides Brazil.

The idea was to bring young women and men together to further explore issues of gender, relationships, sexuality, and health, and to have them promote healthy messages to other young people about these issues. The Entre Nós programme's main medium for sharing these messages is via radio dramas that explore relationships between the sexes, both heterosexual and same-sex dynamics. Their message is also transmitted through community events, comic books, peer-led workshops and promotional materials for young people.

Entre Nós highlights the value of addressing gender dynamics with mixed-sex groups of youth. By bringing young men and women together, they are able to share different perspectives of what it is like to experience something as male or female. Such efforts also help build empathy and understanding for the challenges that members of the other sex face. There is particular value in working with younger people, where gender norms are often viewed as more fluid and relationship skills are just being developed.[78]

The challenge in both health and education is to find ways of supporting girls and women that do not exclude boys and young men, but embrace their different needs in the broader framework of promoting a more equal world.

In the next chapter, we look at how the ways in which men and women are viewed play out in the world of work.

5 | GIVING UP POWER? WOMEN, MEN AND WORK

Jobs for the girls?

This chapter does not start with a story, because, unlike in other areas, there are very few examples of men who are prepared to give up power at work in order to advance women's rights. And yet paid work outside the home is one major area where men continue to hold almost all the power. Men's experience of power here may be contradictory, as we have seen in earlier chapters, but it is less so at work than perhaps in any other area of their lives. Even men who support gender equality and feminism tend to shy away from addressing the huge differentials that remain in the workplace, perhaps because it is the norms around men as providers (and women's role being in the home) which remain the most deeply entrenched. And it is precisely because of this that challenging them is so important; if men cannot take a feminist perspective on supporting women's paid employment, then we will never achieve gender equality.

This chapter focuses first on the differences between men and women in the workplace, because there have been moves to assert that this is no longer an issue. For example, American author Hanna Roisin, in her book *The End of Men – and the Rise of Women*, claims that: 'The modern economy is becoming a place where women hold the cards.'[1]

And it is true that there have been huge changes for women in terms of employment in the past decades, with women moving into paid employment outside the home in ways that their grandmothers and even their mothers could only dream of. In the USA, for the first time, in 2011, women made up slightly more than half the workforce (owing at least in part to men losing more jobs than women in the 2008–10 recession).[2] There are (some) high-profile women chief executives. There is a small but increasing number of female presidents. Women are moving into jobs that used to be done by men, such as in the pharmaceutical industry. Even those women working in factories or sweatshops, as social economist Naila Kabeer noted, have more choice and independence than if they remained at home.[3] But their experience is contradictory, as feminist economist Ruth Pearson points out: 'As individual workers they experienced both the liberating or the "empowering" impact of earning a regular wage, and of having increased autonomy over their economic lives; at the same time many were also very well aware of the fact that their work was low paid, both in comparison to male workers but also to women workers employed in industrialized countries.'[4]

This contradiction is widespread – although more women are working, they are often still worse paid than men, in part-time jobs or in the huge informal employment sector with little protection and few rights. In many places, the increase in women working is simply driven by the necessity of having two wages to make ends meet.

And at the top of industry and government, the faces remain stubbornly male. In fact, there is some evidence that the numbers of women are actually decreasing. As Sheryl Sandberg, Chief Operating Officer of Facebook, said: 'Women are not making it to the top of any profession in the world.'[5]

This chapter reveals where women really stand in the world of work. It looks at the contradiction between the numbers of women working outside the home and the reasons why they have so little power and are paid less than men. It examines some of the reasons, perhaps most importantly, for the continuing importance of the idea of the role of men as 'provider' of the household to men and women of all backgrounds and in most countries. It explains how this disadvantages men as well as women – as American author and historian Stephanie Coontz points out: 'Social and economic policies constructed around the male breadwinner model have always disadvantaged women. But today they are dragging down millions of men as well.'[6]

The chapter argues that that there will never be economic empowerment for women as long as they are still doing the majority of childcare and domestic work as well as working long hours outside the home. This will not change unless men are prepared not only to share tasks at home, but to give up some of their power and their entrenched views about men and paid work. Finally, it looks at the men who have become engaged in working for equality at work as well as at home, and examines the strategies that will really ensure that 'economic empowerment' for women is translated into promoting economic justice for all.

Working women, working men

It is true that progress in terms of gender equality is uneven, but the proponents of the argument that women are taking over the world at work need only look at statistics on employment, equal pay and political representation of men and women to see just how wrong they are.

Gender analyses of labour markets tend to look at women's participation in paid employment compared with men's – and not the huge informal sector in which so many women work; selling a handful of tomatoes that they have grown in their gardens, picking cotton, or sewing at night long after their children have gone to bed. The number of women owning small and medium-sized businesses is estimated to be between eight and ten million, and although this is still far fewer than that for men owning similar enterprises, numbers are slowly growing.[7] In most countries, the informal sector is far larger than the formal one. For example, in South Asia more than 80 per cent of men and women work in the informal sector, and in sub-Saharan Africa it is 74 per cent of women and 61 per cent of men.[8]

There are also more women in formal paid work today than at any point in history. They now make up about 40 per cent of the global formal labour force,[9] and 43 per cent of the agricultural labour force, although this varies considerably from country to country. For example, in the Middle East and North Africa in 2010, only 21 per cent of women participated in the formal labour market, compared with 71 per cent in East Asia and the Pacific.[10] Men's labour participation rates tend to be more stable, both across countries and in different income groups.[11]

While they cannot be said to be representative, the highest positions are even more elusive for women: only seven of 150 elected heads of state in the world are women, and only eleven of 192 heads of government. The situation is similar at the level of local government: female elected councillors are under-represented in all regions of the world and women mayors even more so. And many of the women in top positions are already lined up for success. The few women in the Forbes rich list mostly come from rich families or business dynasties such as Walmart or Apple.[12]

In the private sector, women are on most boards of directors of large companies but their number remains low compared to that for men. Furthermore, the 'glass ceiling' has hindered women's access to leadership positions in private companies.

This is especially notable in the largest corporations, which remain male dominated. Of the 500 largest corporations in the USA, only twenty-three currently have a female chief executive officer. That is just 4.6 per cent.[13]

Even in the twenty-seven member countries of the European Union, in April 2013 women accounted for only 16.6 per cent of board members of large publicly listed companies. This is up by 5 per cent since October 2010, when the European Commission announced that it was considering 'targeted initiatives to get more women into decision-making positions'. But one in four big companies still have no women on the board at all, and the target of 40 per cent by 2020 is still a long way off.[14] Although there is little data on women managers in the global South, one paper on the subject in Africa notes that: 'The few figures available showed wide disparities, with Egypt at one end of the spectrum with only 10 per cent of managers being women, while Botswana at the top end had 30 per cent.'[15]

Globally, research by accountancy firm Grant Thornton in 2013 found that women now fill 24 per cent of senior management roles, a percentage that is gradually creeping up. But women make up only 16 per cent of board members in the rich-world G7 economies compared with 26 per cent in the BRIC economies (Brazil, Russia, India and China) and 38 per cent in the Baltic countries.[16] Interestingly, as we will see later in this chapter, one possible reason for this is that women in the latter have more access to childcare from extended families or from women they employ as nannies.

This means that in Japan, 93 out of every 100 people in top positions are men, in the USA this is 80 out of 100, and even in the countries at the top of the list, only China has more women than men, and this is a leap from 25 per cent the previous year.

	Top 10 countries	
1	China	51
2	Poland	48
3	Latvia	43
4	Estonia	40
5	Lithuania	40
6	Philippines	37
7	Georgia	37
8	Thailand	36
9	Vietnam	33
10	Botswana	32
	Bottom 10 countries	
1	Spain	21
2	Ireland	21
3	USA	20
4	UK	19
5	India	19
6	Argentina	18
7	Switzerland	14
8	The Netherlands	11
9	United Arab Emirates	11
10	Japan	7

6 Percentage of women in senior management around the world[17]

And interestingly, despite many years of legislation for gender equality, Sweden and Norway are only 27 and 22 in the ranking of top countries.

Women don't have power in other areas either – even in 2013, they still made up only 21.4 per cent of parliamentarians.[18] Most recent figures show that 17.2 per cent of ministerial posts worldwide are held by women – up from 16.1 per cent in 2008, which shows just how slow progress can be.[19]

Lack of political voice is critical given that this is where laws and policies that affect whole populations – both male and female – are made. In the UK, Dame Helena Kennedy, QC, noted in a speech on International Women's Day: 'You don't have to believe in patriarchy to realize that the law was made by men and is dominated by men, and that the same goes for parliament. Which means that in all the making of the law, women are largely absent. It is not surprising that the law doesn't work for women.'[20]

Women who are in powerful positions often find they face a daily barrage of sexist behaviour from men which in many countries is outlawed in the workplace. And often, even among the elite, women do not do as well as men. Eighty-eight per cent of women aged thirty to thirty-nine see their earnings decline when they have children.[21] A study of Harvard graduates in the USA found that 'Median earnings in 2005 were $90K for women but $162.5K for men. Among full-time full-year workers, median earnings were $112.5K for women and $187.5K for men.' The study notes: 'These are not average workers, not even typical college graduates, and the gender gap in earnings is extremely large despite the fact that women in the sample earned considerable amounts.'[22]

What is interesting too is that despite the fact that in many countries girls are forging ahead of boys when it comes to educational attainment, this doesn't always pay dividends when it comes to employment. Despite the youth bulge in much of the global South, even secondary and university education, where girls and young women are excelling, are failing to translate into employment for many young women. As one report from the World Bank notes: 'Progress in education is not matched by higher labour force participation. By age 24, women lag behind in all regions. In Latin America and the Caribbean, the gap is around 26 percentage points. The gap is even larger in South

Asia, where 82 per cent of men are active in the labour market, against just 28 per cent of women.'[23]

If we look at the gender pay gap, the story is no better. An International Labour Organization (ILO) study of eighty-three countries found that women earn between 10 and 30 per cent less than men.[24] Even in the USA in 2010, women working full-time still earned only 77 per cent of the male wage.[25] In sub-Saharan Africa and East Asia and the Pacific, young women aged fifteen to twenty-four who are working earn only 82 and 84 per cent respectively of the amount young men earn in an hour.[26] Accord-

---

Gender and the global economic crisis in the UK

Overall, the economic crisis seems to be affecting women and men differently, because in many countries they tend to be employed in different kinds of industries and on different kinds of contracts. In the UK, Ceri Goddard, chief executive of the Fawcett Society, says the recession means:

> we risk returning to a much more male dominated
> labour market, with record numbers of women
> unemployed, those in work typically earning less, and
> the gap in pay between women and men beginning to
> grow instead of shrink. If women continue to make
> up the majority of those that lose their jobs, but the
> minority of those being hired in new roles, the strides
> women have made in the workplace in the last half
> a century risk being undermined just when women,
> the families many of them support, and our economy
> need them more than ever.[27]

ing to the ILO, if present trends continue, it will be another seventy-five years before the principle of equal pay for work of equal value is achieved.[28]

In some countries, however, in Latin America and the Caribbean and Europe and Central Asia, young women are beginning to earn the same and sometimes even slightly more than young men. And younger women everywhere seem to be doing slightly better in terms of earnings than older women, except in Latin America and the Caribbean, perhaps owing to progress in female education, but also probably because older women have taken

---

Women's unemployment has risen to a twenty-six-year high while men's is decreasing.

- Government plans for growth are leaving women behind: 60 per cent of 'new' private sector jobs have gone to men
- Almost three times as many women as men have become 'long-term' unemployed in the last two and a half years – 103,000 women in comparison to 37,000 men
- If the current pattern of women making up the majority of those losing their jobs but the minority of those benefiting from new employment opportunities continues, the worst-case scenario would see some 1.48 million women unemployed by 2018
- Failure to take more action risks creating a 'female-unfriendly' labour market characterized by persistent and rising levels of women's unemployment; diminishing pay levels for women, and a widening of the gender pay gap[29]

time out to have children while younger women have not.[30] Or because the pay gap is such that in many countries, including, for example, Brazil, middle-class women in paid work outside the home have been able to afford to pay other, poorer women to care for their children.

The cost of women not being engaged in paid work is huge: according to one report the economic cost of failing to educate girls to the same standard as boys in sixty-five low- and middle-income countries was estimated at $92 billion a year.[31] And according to the IMF, whole economies are losing out – if women and men had more equality at work, it would increase GDP (gross domestic product) in the USA by 5 per cent, in Japan by 9 per cent and in Egypt by 34 per cent.[32]

None of this would seem to back up Hanna Roisin's theory that the world of work is becoming a place where 'women hold all the cards'.[33]

Work is almost everything: the old architecture of manliness

Paid work outside the home, in almost every culture, has traditionally been seen as men's domain – even though in reality poor women have always had to earn a living as best they can. In many societies, men may not be the sole providers, but are responsible for overall security and protection. In rural societies, household tasks are divided between people of different ages and gender, with women often responsible for domestic food production, small animals and cash for household essentials. And of course, millions of women are responsible for large extended families where a man is no longer present.

The idea that the man provides while the woman stays at home and does the 'invisible' unpaid work, and that this is the model in most of the world, was challenged in the 1960s and

1970s by feminists in Europe and North America. They questioned the idea that women were 'non-productive' because they were in the home, showed how essential this work was, and argued for a redefinition of care work.[34] In addition, they showed how the nuclear stereotype belied the reality of life in many countries in the South and failed to take into account the huge diversity of family life. This included not only polygamous families, but also cultures where women are in charge of food production or situations where extended families – women, men, children, grandparents, aunts, uncles – all have to work because that is the only way to survive.

Despite these realities in much of the world, the overall perception in most cultures today is still likely to be that providing is the man's role. 'Work and producing income are the key requisites for being a man in most cultures,' says masculinities expert Gary Barker.[35] And despite rising unemployment in the formal sector for both sexes, the trend of women joining the labour market in large numbers is here to stay. So what does this mean for men? Barker notes that when the role of provider is taken away from men: 'The risk of not fulfilling this role is to be reminded that one is not a "true man". ... Since most societies define a man's principal role to be the breadwinner, men face considerable stress when they are not able to fulfil that function.'[36]

Work is almost everything: young men and work[37]

These examples of young men talking about what work means to them show just how central it remains in their lives – even and perhaps especially when they are un- employed.

- '[Work isn't] everything, but almost everything. You know [if you work] you have some money in your pocket. I mean if you don't have work, you see men get involved in all kinds of trouble ... When you have work, you're better off, better for yourself, and nobody wishes you a hard time.' (Anderson, twenty-one, African Brazilian, Rio de Janeiro)
- '[When a man is out of work] ... he's gonna lose control, start to rob, do whatever he can to get money ... if I go out to try to get a job and I don't find it and I see there's all kind of things we need at home that I can't get ... then your mind starts to change ... I mean unemployment is rough.' (Jeferson, nineteen, African Brazilian, Rio de Janiero)
- 'I can't get married now because I can only get married when I have money. The moment I get money, I will get married.' (Adeniyi, Nigeria)
- 'Girls only want one thing from you. If you are out of work, they don't want you. You can clean the toilet and care for the baby, but if you are out of work, she don't want you.' (Young African American man, Chicago, USA)
- 'Here you have to work for money and send it home. That's what you do to show that you are a man.' (Momodou, the Gambia)

These young men know that women may also buy into the ideal of the male provider role, feeling that their male partners are useless if they cannot bring in income for the family. We see this clearly in the context of the USA in what Hanna Roisin calls 'Cardboard Man':

> for most of the century men derived their sense of manliness from their work, or their role as head of the family ... Some decades into the twentieth century, those obvious forms of social utility started to fade. Many men in the US were no longer doing physically demanding labour of the traditional kind, and if they were, it was not a job for life. They were working in offices or not working at all, and instead taking out their frustration on the microwave at the 7-Eleven. And as fewer people got married, men were no longer acting as domestic providers, either. They lost the old architecture of manliness, but they have not replaced it with any obvious new one.[38]

The traditional male provider role also gave men all the power, both inside and outside the home. The man played the public role, the wife the private one. Many women were – and still are – dependent on their husbands, as Fatouma, from the Gambia, said: 'We rely on men for our livelihood. We do not own land. Once I leave my father's home to get married, I cannot go back. I have to stay with my husband. If I leave him, where can I go? What will happen to my children?'[39]

This is a wider issue than employment, important though that is. In many countries in the South, women's lack of landownership, lack of rights to children and inheritance, lack of right to live alone and the requirement for male protection is their weakness in almost every context.

In some cases, however, women's movement into paid employment has brought about a transformation in economic power between husbands and wives that has had positive consequences, as the ILO notes: 'Better job opportunities have increased many women's independence and resulted in a new status and role in their families and society.'[40]

In the Dominican Republic, I spoke to Beda, who is one of fifty women belonging to a local microcredit group in Barreras, says: 'I feel very proud that I am part of this group. It is good for a woman to have her own money.' Ronnie, the group secretary, says: 'It was important to organise a group like this because before so many women stayed home and would have to wait for their husband to bring the money home but now we don't have to do this. We have more security now – the amounts are small but the pot grows. We don't have to worry so much about something happening ...'

But for the woman to be the breadwinner in a society where this has been the man's role can be problematic. The women of Barreras say that they haven't faced any resistance from the men, because often they are using the loans to help the family business – buying nets for fishing, for example. Ronnie says: 'We believe that relationships between husbands and wives are also improving – before, men believed that women had to stay in the house – now it is not so easy for men to say "I am the macho man."'

Not very far away, a group of men gathered to work on masculinities issues told me that the fact that women are earning – and many have migrated to work abroad or in the big cities where the work is – reverses what are seen as traditional gender roles. Women go abroad and learn about equality, and come back with new ideas. Cristobal says that it is all quite confusing: 'We know that this is the world we hope for and work for. But we also worry that if women are educated and know what is a better life, they might leave their husbands.'

Rudio adds: 'Most women still depend on men for money – if

she works she doesn't need money from her husband ...' Some men, he says, don't want women even to be educated: 'If a girl studies, some men worry that she will become superior to them.' Cristobal agrees: 'If there is women's liberation it is a shock for men's reality. And that is how the violence gets worse.' Manuel explains: 'When women exercise their rights today, men are not educated about those rights. So when a woman starts to demand her rights, men get angry. Men need to know how to change their way of thinking.'[41]

The 'sticky floor' – and poor man's patriarchy

The issue of employment must be looked at not just through the lens of gender and of age, but also that of class and race. It seems that women in employment all over the world, whatever class they come from, suffer from the glass ceiling and a gender pay gap – or are simply trying to earn a living selling potatoes in the market or sewing clothes at home. Poor women in particular are often in badly paid, dead-end, part-time jobs, listed by the ILO as 'vulnerable employment'. The ILO refers to 'the sticky floor' – in most countries in the world, women remain the majority in the lowest-paid, least secure jobs, jobs that, as we will see in the next section, are likely to be the most vulnerable in a crisis. For example, in Chile 75 per cent of women in the agricultural sector are hired on temporary contracts picking fruit, and put in more than sixty hours a week during the season. One in three still earns below the minimum wage.[42] In the run-up to the 2012 Olympics in London, a study by War on Want found that, in Bangladesh, five out of six factories making goods for Adidas, Nike and Puma 'did not even pay their workers the Bangladeshi minimum wage, let alone a living wage that allowed them to meet their basic needs. On average workers were paid just 16p an hour, with two thirds of the workers working over 60 hours a week, in clear breach of Bangladeshi law.' The report noted that: 'The burden of long hours falls especially hard on women workers. They carry the burden of unpaid domestic work which has to be completed before and after their shift. They also experience long periods of separation from their children and families.'[43]

What is perhaps less discussed, however, is that poor and working-class men are also perhaps in thrall to patriarchal ways of thinking – and yet have least to gain from them. A four-year study on the effects of food price fluctuations by the Institute of Development Studies in Sussex, in collaboration with Oxfam and research partners in Bolivia, Guatemala, Burkina Faso, Ethiopia, Kenya, Bangladesh, Indonesia, Pakistan and Vietnam,[44] revealed what Naomi Hossain, research fellow, calls a 'poor man's patriarchy'.

Hossain notes that:

The majority of men – men on low and precarious incomes – at present enjoy relatively limited privileges of a patriarchal system, or at least considerably fewer such privileges than they relatively recently did. And while the privileges seem somewhat fewer, the burdens appear greater. This means theirs is a poor man's patriarchy in the double sense: a set of rules about male rights and responsibilities govern the lives of men living in or near poverty, but both the rights and the responsibilities are weakly adhered to in a watery version of a masculinity that revolved (in the recent past), should revolve or does revolve (in many cultural systems, to date) around the idea of the male breadwinner or provider.

The project shows that food price volatility affects poor women too, especially as they may have to find new ways to bring in income. This often means their mothers or older daughters have to replace the work they do in the home – with a knock-on effect on girls' education. It also has an effect on men: the loss of their traditional role as provider can lead to them using violence or deserting their families.

But Hossain also notes in her paper that even, or perhaps particularly, in times of crisis:

> there is also emancipatory potential, most plainly for women, but also for poor men who have less invested in old school patriarchy than before (and indeed, than richer men). There is, perhaps, some basis for cross-gender solidarity in an emancipatory project that prioritises the protection of care or social reproduction without forcing women into the roles of unpaid, unacknowledged carers.[45]

Double shift, triple burden

Crucially, while women have been moving into paid employment, they are still doing the same amount of unpaid work and childcare in the home. Until men and women share the unpaid work, women will still be doing the double shift that makes it difficult to move up the career ladder. This becomes particularly true once they have children, although of course household arrangements are becoming ever more diverse, and roles may be hugely different in some cultures.

Magdalena Sepúlveda Carmona, the United Nations special rapporteur on extreme poverty and human rights, argued in a report in August 2013 that the unequal care responsibilities heaped on women were a 'major barrier to gender equality and to women's equal enjoyment of human rights. In many cases, millions of women still find that poverty is their reward for a lifetime spent caring, and unpaid care provision by women and girls is still treated as an infinite cost-free resource that fills the gaps when public services are not available or accessible.'[46] In a world where those countries with a social welfare system are looking at substantial cuts, this becomes increasingly a concern for everyone.

In a 2006 survey at Princeton University in the USA, 62 per cent of women said they anticipated work/family conflict, compared with 33 per cent of men – and of the men who expected a conflict, 46 per cent expected that their wives would step away from their career track. These expectations yield predictable results: among professional women who take time off for family, only 40 per cent return to work full-time.[47]

Many companies structure their workers' days around the expectation that someone else is handling the home front. Even where men have welcomed women into the workplace, house-work, cooking and child-rearing duties are still borne largely by women. A survey by consultancy McKinsey found that men are promoted based on their potential, while for women promotion is based on past achievements.[48]

In some countries, women (for it is still their problem) have found another solution: get someone else to do the work in the home. Recent research on women in senior management in the emerging BRIC countries (Brazil, Russia, India, China) found that this directly correlated with being able to go back to work when children are young. 'We found, for instance, in India, that the combination of ... extended family and low-cost domestic help meant that child care was really not a problem,' says Sylvia Ann Hewlett, one of the researchers. 'Women in the BRIC countries are able to return to work sooner after having children, while many women in the U.S. disengage from the workforce completely while their children are young. That means that they lose about 18 percent of their earning power permanently, because it's so hard to get back in.'[49] So rather than looking to a male partner or husband (if there is one) to share these tasks, middle-class women with means would rather hand them on – by paying another woman.

The issue of women's domestic work (and men's minimal contribution to this) is studied in more detail in the chapter on fatherhood and caring work. This project in Nicaragua provides a different model – valuing unpaid work in the home as much as paid work outside.

Fair pay for domestic work in Nicaragua

You no longer have to lower your head and wait for the man to tell you what to do; now we make our own decisions and share activities and responsibilities with our partners. (Adilia Amador Sevilla from Achuapa, Nicaragua)

An innovative development is currently taking place in Nicaragua. A number of co-operatives with Fair Trade contracts are including in the costs of production (for sesame oil and green coffee) a component for the unpaid work of women. This is exceptional in a world which consistently undervalues women's work and refuses either to measure it or count it as economic activity, despite feminist campaigning over several decades. The money raised is being used by the co-operatives for collective projects to empower women and improve gender balance in the wider community. As Adilia says, the relations between men and women are being radically altered.

The starting point came in 2008, when the cooperative Juan Francisco Paz Silva needed to renew its Community Trade (equivalent to Fair Trade) contract for sesame oil with the Body Shop. The co-op and ETICO (an ethical trading company that works closely with the co-op) both had strong gender policies and were looking for ways of supporting women through this contract. The idea of including a component for women's unpaid work came as a flash of inspiration, as a recognition and recompense for the contribution to production made by women.

This calculation, and its addition to the costs, was accepted by the Body Shop, although they wanted more justification and more detail on what was actually being paid for. Subsequently some coffee buyers have also agreed to make a similar addition.

Since this development started, there have been more women than men joining the co-ops as new members, an increase in the numbers of women initiating new projects, and a remarkable 100-per-cent payback rate on loans made to women.

These changes have led to an increased sense of self-esteem among the women, who now have greater confidence to speak and participate in the affairs of the co-operatives.[50]

Leaning in?

The other explanation given for why women do not become CEOs is that, from a young age, they are taught not to push themselves forward, while boys are trained to be assertive. The most controversial exposition of this argument came in the book written in 2013 by Sheryl Sandberg, Chief Operating Officer at Facebook, *Lean In: women, work and the will to lead*, in which she argues that: 'In addition to the external barriers erected by society [and she fully acknowledges these] women are hindered by barriers that exist within ourselves.'[51]

In their book *Women Don't Ask: Negotiation and the Gender Divide* (2003), Linda Babcock and Sarah Laschever found that one of the reasons why women fare less well in the labour market than men is that they don't like to negotiate. Men are four times more likely than women to negotiate their salary, and this can make a difference of a million dollars over a lifetime. Sometimes women don't know they can ask, or are afraid of upsetting their boss, partner or colleagues.

Sandberg was criticized by other women (not many men spoke up on this one) for blaming women for their lack of success, but in fact the book is quite clear about the other culprit: 'It has been more than two decades since I entered the workforce, and so much is still the same. It is time for us to face the fact that our revolution has stalled. The promise of equality is not the same as true equality. A truly equal world would be one where women ran half our countries and companies and men ran half our homes.'

But it is not just men who may block women's rise to the top jobs. A 2014 report by accountancy firm McKinsey notes that: 'the results indicate that collective, cultural factors at work are more than twice as likely as individual factors to link to women's confidence that they can reach top management'. They note too that men are much less likely than women to see just how difficult it is for women to reach top management posts: 'While three-quarters of men agree that diverse leadership teams with significant numbers of women generate better company performance, fewer recognize the corporate challenges that women face. Just 19 percent of male respondents strongly agree that reaching top management is harder for women, and they are almost six times more likely than women to *disagree*.'[52] One of the recommendations of the report is for more male sponsorship of women.

Patriarchy in the workplace is supported by women as well as by men – not all women are supportive of their younger peers, as young Australian entrepreneur Holly Ransom points out: 'In my discussions with young women around Australia, the challenges they face with older women in the workforce (ranging from passive lack of support through to active bullying) is one of the most frequent topics of conversation ... The lack of support sourced from the "sisterhood" is exacerbated by the comparative strength of male dominated networks.'[53] So having women in positions of power is a first step, but ensuring that they help their sisters is another, equally important one.

Sandberg's idea of 'leaning in' has been taken up in some unlikely places. In China, for example, women have started 'Lean in' circles. Carrie Huang, aged twenty-one, set up a circle at Renmin University of China, where she studies finance. 'My friends and I, we all felt that we do that – we underestimate ourselves,' she said in an interview.

It has to do with our education and background. Our parents tell us, 'You are girls, get yourself a stable life and don't have too much ambition.' Although women, mainly in cities, are beginning to do better than men at college – Ms. Huang said that there were sixteen women and seven men in her finance class, they still don't believe they are as good as their male peers: 'We lack confidence,' Ms. Huang said, adding that many women in China prioritize their boyfriends' or husbands' goals. 'What we need is the courage to try different things,' she said. 'It's about discovering what you want to do. Parents have wishes for us, and it's hard to change.' Feng Yuan, an activist for gender rights and equality said: 'I don't think the personal approach can change the fundamentally unequal gender structures ... But in terms of a woman's individual situation, it's useful because a lot of women fear feminism, that kind of collective call. A personal message is workable.'[54]

From individual action to collective change

So what will improve women's equal participation in employment? It is important to note here that the solutions do not just lie, as Sheryl Sandberg suggests, with individual women, or indeed with individual men. Nor is it just up to employers, although the measures that they can take, as we see in the Australian study overleaf, are important. And although legislation is important, it too is not enough on its own.

As social economist Naila Kabeer points out, gender inequality in the marketplace is, according to feminist economists, 'structured into market forces by discriminatory practices inherited from the past as well as by the bargaining power exercised in the present by powerful market actors pursuing their own self-interest'.[55] It is on all three fronts therefore – individual, institutional and structural – that discrimination against women in the workplace needs to be addressed.

So what factors encourage women to work in certain professions and what deters them? A paper by gender and development experts Tina Wallace and Helen Baños-Smith that drew from a survey of public sector women across many countries found that it was both policies and attitudes which stopped women attaining more senior positions. Although childcare was the number-one reason, other disincentives were male norms that make life in the workplace uncomfortable for women – such as the lack of 'old boy' networks to support women at work, the fact that they were in a minority and there were few role models, and their lack of time for extra training because of domestic responsibilities.[56]

Wallace and Baños-Smith also looked at the strategies women in senior management in Africa used for support and found that, for example, in Ghana, 'women participants in a University study said attributes such as perseverance, the ability to plan, and their determination to succeed aided them in their struggle to advance'.[57] In South Africa, another study found there was a difference between black women, who said 'their collective strength was drawn from their feminism, personal and social resources (partners, children, female friends)', and white women, who 'relied on friends, faith, and eating to help them to cope'.[58]

A survey by online job marketplace Elance of 7,000 men and women in the tech industry in the USA found that lack of female role models and stereotypes of 'geeks' were deterrents for women, while incentives were equal pay, more inspiration at a young age, more female role models and dispelling stereotypes.[59]

In one survey in Australia, respondents were asked to rank the barriers to women's equality in the workplace.[60] The results were:

1   Workplace culture
2   Lack of female leaders
3   Gender stereotypes
4   Lack of flexible work practices
5   Affordability and accessibility of childcare

6 Sexism

7 Lack of mentors

8 Societal expectations regarding gender roles (e.g. household work/childcare)

Other recurring barriers included:

- Entrenched boys' club, the all-male work environment and macho behaviour;
- Workplace design including the one-income-earner household model and logistics of school and work hours;
- The confusion between 'presenteeism' and commitment, the association of flexible work with lack of commitment, and the lack of career advancement for part-time employees;
- The difficulty in juggling work and personal life, particularly caring responsibilities for children and aged parents;
- The lack of support among women, women's lack of self-confidence and lack of sponsorship for women in workplaces;
- Unconscious bias;
- Lack of commitment from leaders and executive teams towards gender diversity.

These ideas include a variety of structural and individual changes which are much broader than the 'Lean-in' approach advocated by Sheryl Sandberg. Interesting too that it doesn't mention sexual harassment, which is still such an inhibiting factor that many women over the years have dared not – and still dare not – speak out against it. 'Sexual harassment is all about power,' says British journalist Polly Toynbee, citing the way that groping and worse used to be common currency, until a number of brave women spoke out in employment tribunals. At least men should now know sexual harassment is wrong and that there may be a price to pay. Toynbee continues: 'Touching up women

	Disagree	Agree
India	16	84
Pakistan	14	82
Nigeria	21	77
Egypt	20	75
Indonesia	27	74
China	26	73
Jordan	30	68
Turkey	30	67
South Korea	39	60
Lebanon	49	51
Russia	49	47
Kenya	53	46
Poland	51	44
Argentina	56	43
Japan	58	41
Brazil	63	37
Mexico	69	28
France	80	20
Germany	80	19
USA	85	14
Britain	85	12
Spain	87	12

7 When jobs are scarce, men should have more right to a job[61]

at work is a way to exert power, often an act of aggression to keep them in their place: underneath it all, women's realm is the bedroom. The politics of sex are too difficult to navigate, men complain. At work, as at home, the only etiquette question is who has the power.'[62]

Having money gives you power, which is why it is also a key element in the way that women's work is viewed and valued. 'Men's higher labour force participation relative to women in most regions of the world reflects the breadwinning responsibilities ascribed to them in most cultures,' says Naila Kabeer.[63] A poll by the Pew Research Center[64] found that when asked to agree or disagree with the statement 'when jobs are scarce, men should have more right to a job', 84 per cent of respondents in India agreed, compared with 51 per cent in Lebanon, 47 per cent in Russia, 37 per cent in Brazil, 14 per cent in the USA, and 12 per cent in Britain and Spain.

In some countries, noted an earlier Pew report: 'male respondents are considerably more likely than female respondents to agree that men should have more right to a job than women when jobs are scarce'. It gives the example of Egypt, where nine out of ten men and six out of ten women share this view.[65]

In most countries, the majority of respondents to this same report agreed that women should be able to work outside the home. However, here too there was a big gender gap in some countries. Asked whether they 'completely agreed' that women should be able to work outside home, in eight countries – Pakistan, Egypt, Jordan, Kenya, South Korea, Spain, Lebanon and Indonesia – there was a more than ten-point gap between the opinions of women and men.

One study in Beirut found that 74 per cent of the women said they thought 'domestic work was obligatory even when they worked outside the home', and 85 per cent of men agreed that 'the normal of role of the woman is at home and she cannot do some of the work outside the borders of the home'.[66]

It is clear that gender norms in this area remain very rigid in many countries. So if we relate this back to the idea of men being involved in feminism, in this case as partners or allies in women's economic empowerment, then the question is: what kind of strategies will change this in order to ensure that 'economic empowerment' is translated into promoting economic justice – for women and men?

American critical theorist Nancy Fraser, in her book *Fortunes of Feminism: From State-managed Capitalism to Neoliberal Crisis*,[67] outlines how she believes change is possible, and she proposes giving more value to unwaged work, including care work. This harks back to the earlier controversial feminist 'wages for housework' campaigns which seem to have long since been forgotten.[68]

And while Fraser does not go this far, this might also give impetus to campaigns like MenCare, which is pushing for men to become more involved in childcare and work in the home, arguing that this will mean more women working for pay outside the home because: 'The fact that women do most of the care work is one of the key reasons that women's wages are lower than men even when they work in the same kinds of jobs.'[69]

As yet there are few projects or programmes that explore the links between women's economic empowerment and men's involvement in the home, or that are looking at how care in the home is viewed and valued. One such project is in Rwanda, where Instituto Promundo and the Rwandan Men's Resource Centre (RWAMREC) set up a pilot project with CARE which aimed to explore ways of engaging men in the Village Savings and Loans (VSL) programmes that CARE was running to empower women.[70] The pilot looked at what men thought about women's participation in these programmes, and aimed to develop a way of involving men with their partners in discussing any doubts they had.

An evaluation of the pilot found that the resistance men felt to the women being involved in VSL was gradually broken down, with men acknowledging that their wives' VSL work brought in additional income for the whole family, and led to a sharing of the breadwinner role: 'Several men said they had started to collaborate with their wives to repay loans, seeing the loan as being their responsibility as well. One man commented: "We divided the work: I sell bananas and she sells drinks. We could buy electricity in house and now we are charging phones. With that money, we bought goats and I bought a panje [skirt] for my wife."'

This meant that men also began to share care work. As this man said: 'I learned that I can do women's work, and my wife can do man's work.' And another man said: 'Our culture has changed. The assignment I got was to clean outside the house with a broom. But when the neighbours came, I was hiding the broom. They asked me: "what are you doing?" I told them that I am not poisoned. And I kept on doing it.'

Women too saw the changes in their husbands: 'Before, my husband took decisions and I could not say anything. Now we make decisions together. When husband sells a cow, we discuss how to spend that money. I am very happy, everything has changed.' Another woman stated: 'My husband always took VSL money and drank [it] all in the bar. Now he discusses what to do with the money. Now I take VSL loans and my husband helps to pay back the loans.'

The evaluation found that: 'women participants in microcredit programmes need to be supported by improved and better programming which engages with men in deliberate and structured ways, including promoting greater male involvement in care work ... in some settings, solely focusing on women may lead to negative effects for women, both in the short and long term.'[71]

Projects like this one are able, in Fraser's terms, to link the struggle against 'masculinist cultural values' with the campaigns

for economic justice, 'reconnecting the dream of women's liberation with the vision of a solidary society'.[72] But they are a long
way from challenging the powerful men who still control most
of the world's institutions.

As in other areas of women's lives, collective action for change
has been able to effect changes to women's employment, ensuring that legislation is enforced, campaigning for affordable
childcare and social protection, or lobbying for training and
skills development. As Naila Kabeer notes: 'The organisational
capacity of working women, whether they are self-employed or
wage workers, may be the missing ingredient that can help to
transform women's access to paid work into an economic pathway to empowerment and citizenship.'[73]

There is a wider context too. Women's economic empowerment cannot be seen in isolation from other family members,
be they male or female partners or a wider extended family.
It is therefore also important to understand the dynamics of
couples, families and cooperation, and to look at policies that
take account of the needs of all genders.

Stephanie Coontz, Professor of Family History at Evergreen
State College, points out that this will help men as well:

> Social and economic policies constructed around the male
> breadwinner model have always disadvantaged women. But
> today they are dragging down millions of men as well. Para-
> doxically, putting gender equity issues at the centre of social
> planning would now be in the interests of most men ... It's
> the best way to reverse the increasing economic vulnerability
> of men and women alike. Given the increasing insecurity of
> many American men, they have good reason to back feminist
> policies.[74]

She goes on to argue for reliable, affordable childcare, a living wage for all, improved welfare benefits and unemployment insurance – all of which would benefit men as well as women.

Unfortunately, in many countries, it is precisely these areas that are being cut while inequality increases. As feminist economist Ruth Pearson notes:

> In the current political crisis, in which in the UK and elsewhere women are bearing the brunt of new conservative fiscal policies that see public services as dispensable luxuries for the undeserving poor, it is more important than ever to insist on the importance of the provision of what might be called 'reproductive commons' – that is publicly resourced reproductive labour and services.[75]

In an article in the *New York Times*,[76] Stephanie Coontz points to studies that show that men and women in the USA say they want to share family responsibilities (see Chapter 6) but that: 'When people are caught between the hard place of bad working conditions and the rock wall of politicians' resistance to family-friendly reforms, it is hard to live up to such aspirations.' She concludes: 'Our goal should be to develop work-life policies that enable people to put their gender values into practice. So let's stop arguing about the hard choices women make and help more women and men avoid such hard choices. To do that, we must stop seeing work-family policy as a women's issue and start seeing it as a human rights issue that affects parents, children, partners, singles and elders.'

If women are to make this major shift in favour of equality and justice, then they have much more chance of success if men, who still hold most of the power, are with them rather than against them. There is still a long way to go, but even the singer Beyoncé Knowles, who recently 'came out' to call herself a feminist, is clear that men need to get involved:

> We need to stop buying into the myth about gender equality. It isn't a reality yet. Today, women make up half of the U.S. workforce, but the average working woman earns only 77 percent of what the average working man makes. But unless women and men both say this is unacceptable, things will not change. Men have to demand that their wives, daughters, mothers, and sisters earn more – commensurate with their qualifications and not their gender. Equality will be achieved when men and women are granted equal pay and equal respect.[77]

The next chapter looks at men becoming more involved with their children and in the home. This would also serve to address one of the major barriers to women's advancement in the field of paid employment – their lack of time. At the same time, it would mean that men have to take on and challenge traditional notions of masculinities.

6 | THE FATHERHOOD REVOLUTION?

Fatherhood and caring

Steven is a father from Sri Lanka. His wife works in the Middle East in order to support their family while Steven stays at home and looks after their two small children.

He was interviewed as part of a film for MenCare, a global campaign for men to be more involved in caring roles,[1] about how he felt after she left.

I noticed the difference at once. The children wouldn't drink their milk. They became thin. When my wife was around I was high and mighty. I wouldn't lift a finger. The food had to be placed in my hand. There is a general perception here that men should not perform the duties of women. Other men had wives who worked abroad and they left their children in the care of relatives. It was suggested that I do the same and lead an easy carefree life like they do. But I felt I had to look after my children.

Initially there was some embarrassment. Especially when I went to the hospital for injections for my children because it was mostly women there. When I told the doctor I was looking after them, he thought I was joking. The children both had high fevers. They put them into two beds and I went to the bathroom and cried. This was a day I would never forget.

After three days they were better. I understood that my feeling down was affecting them. So I started playing with them. I would stay up at night and give them their milk.

Some men would make fun of me. I had grown my hair long and they said I was playing the role of a woman. I would take no notice of them. When I was washing clothes, women would watch me. They would look at me with sympathy. They said the good I was doing would come back to me. Those words hit me in the heart. I found great strength and peace of mind in their encouragement.

There is definitely happiness in just being there. When I carry them and they kiss me, or even when they pull my hair, I get goose bumps. It makes me really happy.

The need to be masculine suddenly disappeared. It felt like a matter of months and something changed inside of me. I know that when my wife returns we will lead a good life.

Now I have realized what wives go through every day. When my wife is doing housework, we'll do it together. My thinking was that I would earn money and everything else was her responsibility. I don't feel that way anymore. Of all the things in the world that money can't buy, one is the love of a child.

Steven is unusual, but he is not alone. The fact that in 2013 the president of the USA is the figurehead for a campaign on responsible fatherhood[2] signals that there may even be a quiet revolution going on. Increasing numbers of men are becoming more involved in looking after their children. In many countries, it is no longer unusual to see a man carrying his baby, or pushing a child in a buggy to the park, or even attending 'mother and toddler' groups. This is a big change from previous generations, when fathers were much more aloof.

Although this is primarily a rich-world revolution, and there are still relatively few studies in the South, a study by Instituto Promundo and the International Center for Research on Women

(ICRW) in six countries – Brazil, Chile, Croatia, India, Mexico and Rwanda – found that between a third and a half of men said they took part in the daily care of their child.[3]

So what is driving this 'fatherhood revolution'? The changes have been strongly influenced by the women's movement, as Australian masculinities expert Michael Flood notes: 'The ideology of fatherhood didn't shift because of the changing behaviour of fathers, but largely in response to shifts in the conduct of motherhood.'[4] Once again, men are changing (slowly) because women have been changing (fast).

The fatherhood revolution is also driven by the changes in relationships. Marital breakdown means that there are more single parents, and some of these are men. It is also due to economic realities, as women like Steven's wife all over the world increasingly move into paid work. For example, in places where more women are working, the number of fathers who stay at home to look after the children seems to be slowly increasing – in Canada, in 2011, 13 per cent of families had a father who stayed home, compared with 4 per cent in 2006. But the actual number of fathers who worked part-time while their spouse worked full-time increased by only 6,555 between 1976 and 2010.[5] So perhaps the word 'revolution' is still a little too strong.

This chapter will look in more detail at this 'revolution' and the contradictions that lie embedded within it. What have been the catalysts for change? What are the actual and potential benefits of involved fathers – for women, for children, and for men themselves?

It will show that despite the dads in the parks, women continue to do the lion's share of domestic work and childcare in most of the world, even when they are working – though men and women sometimes disagree about this. It will look at the fathers' rights movement and how it has come to be linked to an anti-feminist agenda. It will examine what is preventing men being active fathers. And it will conclude that in the end it is a matter of will. As men still hold most of the power, if they really wanted change in their own lives, then they could make it happen.

The courage to raise a child

> We need fathers to realize that responsibility does not end at conception. We need them to realize that what makes you a man is not the ability to have a child – it's the courage to raise one. (US president Barack Obama)[6]

Four out of five men will become fathers at some point in their lives.[7] Discussions about involved fatherhood began as early as the 1970s in the USA. They then matured into the responsible fatherhood movement in the 1980s and 1990s.[8] But it is perhaps in the last ten years that fatherhood has started to be linked to gender equality and to feminism. There is a growing recognition that learning to be a better father can have a positive effect on children, on women and on men themselves.

This was corroborated by the online survey for this report, which found that 54.4 per cent of respondents thought men had become more involved in childcare and housework over the past ten years while only 15.4 per cent thought they had not.

The other shift that is happening is that there has been a rise in the number of children being brought up in very diverse households, often with their birth mother and a new partner, or in some countries by gay parents or adoptive parents. In many countries, the nuclear model was never the norm, and children continue to be brought up by grandparents, aunts and uncles or other relatives. Here too men are often playing a more active role.

All of the above reflects the fact that, in many countries, men are becoming involved with their children in a way that it would have been impossible to imagine for their grandfathers or even their fathers. In the USA, since 1965, fathers have almost tripled the amount of time they spend with their children.[9] In Canada, in 2005, 73 per cent of fathers reported daily participation in childcare, compared with 57 per cent in 1986.[10] In one study of Europe-wide organizations working on men's issues, fatherhood was the second-most important theme – after violence.[11]

A badge of pride: paternity leave

Changes in the law, particularly on paternity leave, have also meant that more fathers are involved with their children, at least in their early months. And research has shown that this can lead to better relationships later on, not only with their sons and daughters but with the mothers of their children as well.[12]

Although paternity leave is paltry compared to maternity leave in most countries, there is change in the global South as well as in the North. For example, although Chile has only five days of paternity leave, a new national policy that encourages women to have a male partner or other person of their choice in the delivery room has meant that 95 per cent of younger men between the ages of eighteen and twenty-four were present at the birth of their child compared with 61 per cent of men between the ages of fifty and fifty-nine. In Thailand, as of March 2013, civil servants can now take fifteen days of paid paternity leave.[13] Brazil not only has significant paid maternity leave up to 180 days (sixty days of which are optional for private companies), but also has five days' paid paternity leave.

In the private sector too, paid paternity leave is becoming more common – Google, Kimberly-Clark, IBM, Merrill Lynch, Microsoft, SAS and Yahoo all have paternity leave policies – though more research is needed on how many new fathers actually take this up. A recent article in the *Atlantic* magazine showed that in the USA at least, support for paternity leave, and recognition of the benefits for men, women and children, was becoming increasingly seen as acceptable.[14] In the UK, a study in 2012 for the private company British Telecom found that two-thirds of men (67 per cent) don't think their employers have sufficient family-friendly policies.[15] Almost nine out of ten said they wanted more support from their employer:

- 49 per cent want to be able to work flexibly;
- 21 per cent want to be able to take paternity leave;
- 25 per cent want their employer to be more understanding of the demands of fatherhood;
- 38 per cent would like support with childcare.

But paternity leave is not the answer for everyone. For families who are not in paid employment, or for the many millions who work in the informal sector, the issue of paternity leave simply does not apply. And where it does, because it is often the man in a heterosexual couple who earns more, if the man takes leave there is often insufficient household income unless his salary is compensated for either by government or by his company. Even where the laws have changed, men are not taking up the offer of leave in large numbers unless it is non-transferable – in Scandinavia, which is probably the flagship, the numbers of men taking paternity leave have increased since the introduction of laws for shared parents' leave (see the box on Sweden opposite). Says Petra Persson, a Swedish economist

Sweden: encouraging involved fatherhood[16]

Sweden is often seen as the model for gender equality, and in terms of encouraging fatherhood it has taken some radical steps. As early as 1974, the six months of allowable maternity leave became parental leave, meaning that fathers as well as mothers could take leave.

In 1995, the government introduced a month's 'daddy quota', which could only be taken by the father. In 2002, this was increased to two months. The strategy worked; while 49 per cent of fathers of children born in 1993, before the introduction of the father's month, did not use any of the parental leave allowance, by 2007 fathers claimed 44 per cent of parental leave.

Parental leave has now increased to sixteen months. There is still a way to go, though. In 2007, only 5 per cent of fathers and mothers shared their parental allowance days equally (40–60 per cent). In July 2008, a gender equality bonus was introduced as an incentive to share the parental allowance more equally. The parent with the lower income (usually the mother) receives a tax deduction of at most €300 for going back to work full-time while the other parent (usually the father) takes parental leave.

at Stanford University, 'Being seen as an equal parent is now a badge of pride for men.'[17]

What women want …

This section looks at how the fatherhood revolution has affected women. The honest answer, especially if we look at it globally, is probably 'very little', but that it does have potential for much wider-reaching change.

In theory at least, if women have fewer domestic responsibilities, they are freed up to work – although of course in many countries, particularly but not only in rural areas, poor and working-class women have always worked. A review of the literature on men and caregiving in 2008 found that: 'Men's participation in domestic chores, including childcare, and their positive participation in child and maternal health is generally positive for women, freeing up time for them to work outside the home, to study or to pursue activities that are generally positive for themselves and their households.'[18]

In the North, a study in Sweden found that a mother's future earnings increase around 7 per cent for every month that the father takes paternity leave.[19] But Sweden is probably the exception rather than the rule when it comes to gender equality. And the problem is also that, in general, women earn less than men. Other factors also make a difference to women's earning potential – for example, research in Argentina found that the probability of women being employed rose between 7 and 14 percentage points if pre-school infrastructure was expanded.[20]

In some countries, the increased confidence that women have as a result of social and economic changes has also led to increased expectations, particularly from those who are young and live in urban areas. In Poland, for example, a World Bank study[21] found that women expected their husbands or partners to 'understand the woman's needs', 'realize that I do not feel like cooking and prefer to go to a restaurant', 'remember the children's birthdays' and 'remember our anniversary [celebrate it] and know how to make the pleasure' (adult women in Dobrowice, Poland). In many countries, young women in particular are no longer happy to have the same unequal relationships with men as their mothers did. And they believe they have as much right to sexual pleasure as a man. In the World Bank study, young women said they wanted to be 'more proactive, less tolerant of abuse, and more informed [than their mothers]'.[22]

In fact, most research reveals that women everywhere are still seen as having the main role at home even if they also do paid work. Men's roles, and men's and women's views of their roles, have changed very little in many countries. And women still do the bulk of the childcare. Even in a country like the USA, they believe this holds them back at work – for example, a recent study by the US-based Pew Research Center found that more than half of working women with children under the age of eighteen said that 'being a working parent has made it harder for them to advance in their job or career', compared with only 16 per cent of men in the same situation.[23]

Opinions on what kind of marriage is preferable – one where the man earns and the woman stays at home, or one that is more egalitarian – are beginning to shift. According to the Pew Research Center's Global Attitudes Project in 2010,[24] in nineteen out of twenty countries, a majority of respondents were in favour of a more egalitarian marriage. Only in Egypt (48 per cent), Jordan (47 per cent) and particularly Pakistan (18 per cent) was there not a majority. The report also noted, however, that 'views of marriage have become more egalitarian since earlier in the decade in seven of the 19 countries for which trends are available. This change has been especially dramatic in Jordan, where the balance of opinion has shifted since 2002; then, 37 per cent of Jordanians opted for a more egalitarian approach, compared with the nearly half who do so now.' It notes that: 'In China, Pakistan and Nigeria, however, views of marriage have become more traditional since 2002.'

In 2011, a study by the Center for Work and Family at Boston College[25] of 963 working fathers found that 65 per cent of the fathers believed that both partners should provide equal amounts of care but only 30 per cent said that caregiving was actually divided equally.

The number of families where both parents work is increasing all the time as more women become involved in paid work. In Canada, for example, the percentage of families with children under sixteen where both parents work increased from 36 per cent in 1976 to 68 per cent in 2010.[26] In the USA, the figure is 60 per cent.[27] And 62 per cent of adults in the USA (72 per cent of those under thirty) say they believe the ideal marriage is one in which husband and wife both work and share childcare and household duties.[28] However, this is not necessarily translating into men and women actually sharing the work at home. The *International Encyclopaedia of Masculinities*, in its entry on 'Fatherhood', notes that: 'there is a resounding consensus across a broad range of literature since the 1980s that there remains a persistent connection between women and the responsibility for children and for domestic and community life even where women have equal participation in paid employment'.[29]

A World Bank study in twenty countries found that although 'women are now 40 per cent of the global workforce and their income has risen relative to men in much of the world ... Men ... are *not* doing 40 per cent of the care-giving and domestic work at the household level. Research from diverse settings in the Global North and South shows that women carry out between two and ten times the amount of care work as men.'[30] Another multi-country study found that women do twice the amount of unpaid care work that men do. In India and other low-income countries it can be up to ten times more.[31]

	Brazil	Chile	Croatia	India	Mexico	Rwanda
Father's report: He plays equal or greater role in daily care of child	60	52	61	16	54	52
Women's report: Male partner plays equal or greater role in daily care of child	26	35	47	18	47	23

8 Men's and women's reports of men's participation in domestic duties, percentage[32]

Women tend to disagree with men on the amount of housework and childcare they say they do, as the IMAGES study in Brazil, Chile, Croatia, India, Mexico and Rwanda shows. While between 16 and 60 per cent of fathers said that they played an equal role in the daily care of their child, the number of mothers who thought this was true was only between 18 and 47 per cent. India was the exception, with both mothers and fathers reporting very low involvement but mothers in fact being slightly more positive than fathers.[33]

In many Western countries, fathers are doing more childcare and housework than they did a decade or two decades ago, but they are still doing less than women. For example, in the USA mothers spend about twice as much time with their children as fathers (13.5 hours per week for mothers in 2011, compared with 7.3 hours for fathers).[34] In Canada, in 2005, mothers still spent more than 5.4 hours a day compared with 3.6 hours for fathers on domestic work.[35] Justine Roberts, co-founder of the website Mumsnet, said: 'In our experience, women still pick up the bulk of the domestic duties in the house – even when both parents are working. It is great that men are getting more involved with the kids, but there's still a big divide on other

The dreaded exercise[36]

Samuel and his wife Florence found their lives changed for the better when they agreed to attend a gender training programme called Positive Masculinities, run by the Rwanda Men's Resource Centre (RWAMREC).

In December last year, Samuel Munyaneza, 45, and his wife Florence Uzamunkunda, 32, finally decided to try the dreaded exercise. For three days Florence would milk the cows and cut the firewood (traditionally a man's job and considered taboo for Rwandan women) and Samuel would cook rice and sweep the courtyard – wifely duties, no doubt. It was a critical step towards resolving their marital discord.

On the first day the husband and wife, who live in Murambi village of Huye district in southern Rwanda, switched chores, they caught the attention of their neighbours. 'They were laughing and mocking me as I fumbled around with the pots. They were the same people who always taunted me that I might kill Florence one day. Or how no amount of *inkwano* (bride money) would ever get me a new woman,' the father-of-three smiles.

'But we had to do it; it was recommended by the trainer,' Florence cuts in. 'Here,' she says, turning her face and running her fingers over her jaw. 'Last time he hit me so hard I couldn't chew for weeks and my eye was swollen shut. He told everyone the cow gored me, but cows don't swear. The neighbours heard everything.' Samuel shifts uneasily.

Strange though it may seem, Florence – married to

Samuel for 14 years – is immensely grateful for the last fight. Today the millet farmer, once notorious for his mercurial temper, is viewed as an opinion leader in his community. A respected elder and role model, Samuel now frequently presides over *umugoroba w'abashakanye* – the evening dialogue sessions in the village with couples facing serious marital disputes including abuse and violence.

Adapted from an article written by Nishtha Chugh, one of the winners of the Guardian's International Development Journalism Competition 2013.

activities with women doing more cooking, reading with kids, activity planning, and homework to name a few, which is why we see so many women still struggling to balance a successful career with family life.'[37]

In addition, women have traditionally felt that the home is the only domain where they have some control, and they may resent men 'interfering' or even feel that having a man 'helping' in the house is like having an additional child – in Nicaragua, one study of mothers of children under two found that women said they had more to do in the home when a father was around than when he was not.[38]

Perhaps this is not surprising, when, as we have seen in the chapter on employment, men still earn more than women and they also work longer hours, which means that it is often the woman who decides to give up work when a child is born – in the USA, professional women whose husbands work more than fifty hours a week are twice as likely as other married mothers to give up work. This rises to more than three times more likely when their husbands work more than sixty hours.[39]

These choices are economic, and as such can lead to resentment from both parties. In an article for the *New York Times*, Stephanie Coontz argues that: 'Today the main barriers to further progress toward gender equity no longer lie in people's personal attitudes and relationships. Instead, structural impediments prevent people from acting on their egalitarian values, forcing men and women into personal accommodations and rationalizations that do not reflect their preferences.' As a result, she says: 'The gender revolution is not in a stall. It has hit a wall.'[40]

... and what men need

'For me, my idea of heaven is in [my] daughter's laughter,' rapper Jay-Z told London's *Metro* newspaper.[41] While most of the evidence is anecdotal, it seems that many men who become more actively involved with their children find that it has a positive impact on their own lives.

The reasons why men decide to be active fathers are complex. Some men are motivated to be there for their children because their own fathers were not there for them. For example, Cristóbal, an older man in the Dominican Republic, told me: 'When I was young my parents treated us like animals. We worked, we never went to school. I wanted to make a different family. I hope now my children will treat their own children differently.'[42]

At the other end of the spectrum, men whose fathers were actively engaged with them when they were small, who changed nappies and did housework, are motivated to do the same when their own children are born. As Figure 9 on page 158 shows, research in Brazil, Chile, Croatia, India, Mexico and Rwanda found

What fathers say

- 'She's [pointing to his daughter] the main reason [I got out of gangs]. I didn't really want this to happen [to be a father] but when she was born I made a promise to myself that I don't want her to go through what I did' (Kique, Chicago).[43]

- 'My life totally changed when I had my children – I learned to respect women and children more and to do more around the house. Having children motivates you to work, not to do wrong things' (Ernesto, Khayletisha township, Cape Town, South Africa).[44]

- 'I am excited about [my wife] being pregnant, I have started to learn about it. I am willing to learn everything – changing nappies ... Most of the time I ask she likes my cooking. I clean too. I want to do everything from the start to infinity!' (Solanzi, about-to-be first-time father, Khayletisha township, Cape Town, South Africa).[45]

- 'Before I had my daughter, I only knew how to play. The money I was able to make was just for me, like for my house and my clothes. Now that I have a daughter, my obligation is to her ... if there's anything missing at home, I have to go after it' (João, young father, Rio de Janeiro).[46]

- 'I want them [my children] to remember that I took care of them, that their father struggled for them to complete school even if he doesn't have a job and is poor' (Father of Jacel, the Philippines).[47]

that: 'According to men's own reports of their practices, younger men, men with more education and men who saw their fathers do domestic work are more likely to carry out domestic duties.'[48]

Although the focus of many development efforts has often been on girls' education, boys' education is also important for changing gender relations. This conclusion was confirmed in another Mexican study, which found that 79 per cent of university-educated men, but only 22 per cent of men with no or low education, thought that women and men should share domestic work.[49] In Mexico, another study of urban men found that those with more education were more likely to participate in domestic work, whatever their income level or employment.[50] In the IMAGES study, men with education were also more likely to be among those who took paternity leave when their babies were born. It also found that men who saw their fathers do domestic work were also more likely to follow their lead when

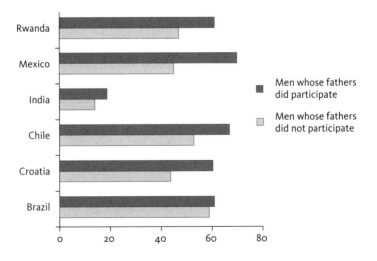

9 Links between fathers' and sons' participation in domestic duties (defined as playing an equal or greater role in one or more duties)[51]

they became adults. There is a real chance that this revolution will start to spread down the generations.

The greatest support: the positive effects of active fathering

Engaged fathers can have a positive impact on their children's lives. If they are involved early on, they are more likely to continue to be involved.[52] The IMAGES study in Brazil, Chile, Croatia, India and Mexico found that between 84.5 per cent (India) and 99.1 per cent (Chile) of fathers who had taken leave after their child was born said that it led to a better relationship later on.[53]

In particular, how a boy is treated by his father is likely to strongly influence how he treats his own children when he grows up. On the negative side (as we will see in the next chapter), being the victim of violence, or watching violence in the family, is one of the main drivers of continuing violence down the generations. On the positive side, one study notes that: 'The more mainstream these ideas [about men and gender equality] become, the easier it is for young men and boys to follow their fathers as role models and be socialized in more egalitarian gender norms.'[54]

Another study on Latin America, while pointing out that most research in this area has been in the West, notes that: 'The consensus from research from Western European and North America ... is that when men (as social fathers or biological fathers) are involved in the lives of children, children benefit in terms of social and emotional development, often perform better in school and have healthier relationships as adults.'

It also goes on to point out that: 'However, this research also affirms that it appears that having multiple caregivers, or having a second caregiver to support a primary caregiver, is more important than the sex of the caregiver per se. Indeed, research

Young, black and proud to be a father[55]

St Michael's Fellowship in London, UK, runs a pioneering project for fathers and fathers-to-be, aged fourteen to twenty-five. Many had absent dads – and are determined to do better for their children.

The family practitioner there is Seany O'Kane, who describes himself as the pied piper of young dads. He goes into nursery schools and maternity wards and encourages young fathers to sign up to his classes. Lessons cover everything from how to keep in regular contact with their children to hands-on skills such as bathing, feeding and changing nappies.

'The overwhelming majority of young men in these classes didn't have fathers around,' says O'Kane. 'So statistically it's easy to say they won't be around for their children. We're here to dispel the myth that they don't want to be part of their children's lives. We as a nation are chastising these young men, saying you aren't good at this – but we aren't giving them the support or the opportunities.'

Jerome Henry, 26, who went there looking for support after becoming a father last summer, was so inspired by what he learned there that he set up a forum for young fathers – an informal group where they could discuss issues. He also organized a walk on Father's Day – The 100 Dads Walk – to represent fathers walking into their children's lives as opposed to walking away. He plans to do the same this year.

'The only thing I had was looking out the window waiting for my dad to turn up and take me to football,' says Jerome. 'He never turned up, and that hurts. I'll never do that to my daughter. There's nothing better than being a father – it's a good feeling. I'm going to be a better dad.'

from the U.S. and other settings – particularly those which are stressed and resource-poor – confirms that having multiple, supportive caregivers, regardless of their sex, is probably the most important protective factor for child well-being.'[56]

There are numerous studies, again mostly in the West, that show the positive effects of active fathering on children, both boys and girls. While the main emphasis of much development literature has been on the positive effects of maternal education on children's education and health, studies in the USA have shown that there are links between how much a father is involved and how well his children do at school. For example, one found that adolescent girls and boys were less likely to fail their grades if they had strong links with a father or stepfather.[57] In North America and Europe, twenty-two out of twenty-four studies found that involved fathers had a positive impact on both sons and daughters, with boys having fewer behavioural problems and girls fewer psychological problems than those with non-involved fathers, and cognitive development for both boys and girls also improving.[58]

In the developing world, fathers have considerable control over resources and often still make the main decisions that affect a family's livelihood, and yet many interventions continue to target solely women, who may not have the authority to put them into practice. The report notes that: 'Fathers' involvement is one of the greatest, yet most underutilized, sources of support available to children in our world today.'[59]

A fairer deal: what prevents men being more involved fathers?

As we saw in Chapter 3, attitudes about men's and women's roles in the family are formed at a very young age. And they do not seem to have changed substantially in the past decade in many countries. For example, focus groups in Brazil with young men for Plan's 2011 'State of the World's Girls' report found that they recognized that the country's macho culture was responsible for the differences in the ways boys and girls were treated. They pointed out that since girls were expected and taught to do housework, this gave them little space to learn: 'The girl is taught to wash clothes since she's very little.' 'If we want to learn we have to go and do it, because we are only taught to play football and other men's activities ...'[60]

A World Bank study in twenty countries noted that: 'income generation for the family was the first and most likely mentioned definition of a man's role in the family and of a good husband':[61]

- 'A good husband is a good provider of things such as food, clothes' (Afghanistan)
- 'A good husband is one who provides for everything in the house. He pays all the bills' (Burkina Faso)
- 'A good husband is one who earns a decent income and keeps his family in good comfort ... He has to be a good provider and has to put in extra hours, if necessary for this purpose' (India)
- 'He should go to his work in the early morning and get money for his children' (North Sudan)

Girls, they found, had changed more than boys: 'for girls, expectations of gender-defining household roles are changing. In their testimonies, the girls themselves redefined housework as a practice that ideally should be normative for both boys and girls, and their [idea of] a good boy reflects that ideal.' However, boys 'are not as eager to include domestic responsibilities in their concept of a good boy'.[62]

In the UK, too, in 2008, 16 per cent of men still agreed that: 'a man's job is to earn money; a woman's job is to look after the home and family' – although twenty years earlier the figure was almost double that.[63] It is still the minority of men who are active fathers. Gideon Burrows, who has recently written a book on men and fathering in the UK, said:[64]

> Traditional views about men and women's roles play a huge part [in why men are not more active fathers]. And those pressures are only cemented when maternity services pretty much ignore fathers, the baby change is always in the women's loos [toilets] and baby groups are routinely advertised for mums and toddlers. At playgroups, I've had women sit at the opposite end of the room to avoid me. Outside the pre-school, some women do little to make men part of their world. Out in town with my kids I'm still asked: are you babysitting today?[65]

In the North, many fathers talk about being the only father in a pre-school group – often known simply as a 'mother and toddler' group. This human resources manager in the private sector in the UK said this perception discouraged men from taking on childcare and meant they felt pressured to do paid work instead: 'I think it's probably tougher for fathers because the sort of impression you get is that women are the people who go and take the kids to the doctor's, they pick them up from school. The mothers have to be more flexible than the fathers in doing that. So there's more pressure for the father to stay in the job, stay there and keep on working.'[66]

And if this is tough in the middle classes of rich countries, it is much more so if you are poor and live in the South. 'Does a good husband have to be a good provider?' asks the facilitator in a focus group in a village in Sudan. 'Yes, that is the main reason why he is the head of the family. You know, if he doesn't do that people will make jokes about him.'[67] 'Imagine my girlfriend and I had a child,' says Dikitso Letshwiti, a young man from Botswana. 'I can already picture the looks on my friends' faces if they saw me with a dirty nappy in my hand. They'd make fun of me. Still, that is how I would want to relate to my child. I want to be a caring dad. That's worth a good belly laugh.'[68]

Men who work in caring professions have even bigger barriers to negotiate, as this twenty-two-year-old daycare provider in Brazil pointed out: 'They [friends] think it's funny ... that a man is disposed to doing those things [in daycare]. Because when you work in a daycare, people don't think of the pedagogical work you're doing. They think you're changing diapers.' Or as this male nurse in India said: 'Male nurses feel a little uncomfortable. The nursing profession is 90 per cent women. It is a little difficult for men to adjust.'[69]

The stereotypes about women are equally persistent: 'the good wife is strictly defined by a long list of submissive qualities and household tasks, including being nurturing and gentle mannered; tending to the house; caring for the children, the husband, and the elderly; cooking well, and also contributing to the household income if and when needed'.[70]

These attitudes may be bolstered by the media. The online survey for this report asked: 'What factors prevent men becoming involved in gender equality?'; 71.5 per cent of respondents cited the media. As one respondent commented: 'Belief that there is nothing wrong and that the status quo is either natural or meritocratic [this is promulgated both by existing culture and media].'

Unfortunately, the media often presents a contradictory view of fatherhood. As Richard Collier, Professor of Law at Newcastle University, says:

> Fatherhood might have undergone a revolution, but it is a messy one ... People write in the press about fatherhood all the time now, but what really strikes me is that you move from a celebration of fatherhood to a devaluing of fatherhood often in the same pages. It is almost as though we have two views of fatherhood in the law – the pessimistic view, if you like: fathers as a social problem – fathers not being responsible, not caring, not changing ... The antidote is the 'new father', the softly spoken, woolly jumper-wearing man, holding the baby with one arm and doing the dishes with the other.[71]

Most men would not want to be seen in either of these categories.

On the other hand, studies of men who have taken on 'caring' roles have found that they adapt and enjoy them. For example, one man in India who had been an engineer but became a primary caregiver said: 'I consciously have decided to get into the role of homemaker ... I just love doing things that I do.' And another noted that for him it was not a challenge because he had been an equal partner in bringing up his son from day one.[72]

Perhaps many men – particularly those in power – don't want it enough? This message is probably better coming from a man than from me as a female and a feminist. Gideon Burrows notes that if they wanted to, the thousands of men in charge of most countries and governments (for it is still mainly men in charge) could make it happen. It is partly about legislation, and about employers being more family friendly for both men and women. But where paternity leave does exist, men mostly don't use it.

In the end, as Burrows says, it is, once again, down to power: 'Men pretty much run the government, most private companies, the public sector and the media. If we really wanted a fairer deal, we could make it happen very quickly. We don't, because it's not in our interests ... The truth is that men don't really want to do childcare, and are successfully using convenient excuses to avoid it.'[73]

This is part of the truth – the other part is that we live in a world where there is increasing competition for paid employment, and men (and women) fear taking time off to care for a family member for fear of losing their status, or even their job. In many places, employment is precarious and taking time off for anything – whether it be ill-health or a sick child or a pregnant partner – is not only not sanctioned but is frowned upon, or is simply not possible because it would mean less money coming into the household. In an increasingly cut-throat environment, this is true whether you are a top executive or a taxi driver. So it is not only attitudes among men (and women) towards involved fatherhood which need to change: it is the whole workplace environment, including legislation and rules and protocols.

Absent fathers

So let's not pretend the story is all rosy. Too many children have violent fathers. Too many grow up without their biological father as part of their lives. A survey in forty-three countries on five continents found that three in ten fathers aged twenty-five to twenty-nine and two in ten aged thirty to thirty-nine do not live with their children.[74] Some still see their fathers, others find other men who serve as father-figures, including older brothers, uncles, cousins, grandfathers, etc. Increasing numbers of children live in complex families with step- or half-siblings and parents. And in many countries, changes in the law have also allowed gay and lesbian couples to have children. But there has been a huge rise in many countries in divorce and separation and, in general, most children still live with their mothers after their parents split up. In the USA and the UK, over half of marriages end in divorce, and within two years of separation two out of three of the children of these divorces no longer see their father.[75]

In South Africa, as part of the legacy of racism and apartheid, many black men had to migrate to find work. Work in the mines or other physical labour was harsh and physically demanding, and men had to become used to hardship and pain and the violence that went with it. They were also away from their families, and this absence has continued in the twenty years since apartheid ended. Although accurate statistics are hard to find, absent fathers are still more likely to be the norm than present fathers. In Khayleitsha in Cape Town, Wiseman told me: 'Out of five [men], three will not have had fathers who were not present.' He went on to say: 'They ask: how can we do something different for our own children?'[76]

Another South African study on young fatherhood noted that: 'Not all fathers are proud to be fathers, and unfortunately not all fathers want to participate in the lives of their children. In fact, most South African men do not seem especially interested in their children. They seldom attend the births of their own, they

Children's views of fathers in South Africa[77]

Interviews by researchers Wendy Smith and Linda Richter found that children had mixed views about their fathers.

The good ...

- 'My dad is really really fun, he does very fun stuff and he's really funny and I don't know what I would do if my dad had to die but he will one day. My dream is to win a Gold Medal in the Olympics for my dad for swimming. I just hope he does not pass away before then. And to me and our family he's the best father in the world.'

- 'He spoils us a lot, he is coming back from Cape Town today. I really don't think my dad and mom will ever get divorced. Just to tell you my best friend in the world is my dad. I love my dad the best in the world.'

- 'My father is the best father to me and my brother. He loves us too much. He loves his wife my mom. He is a very honest person and very protective. My dad I think is one of the strongest men in the world.'

... and the difficult

- 'I would like my dad to get another job because he always goes on these long trips and I miss him very much and when he gets back he is always working and I hope he is safe. My dad is a very nice person and I don't want anything to happen to him.'

- 'My father has 17 children, he not give that children money. ... He sleep with all moms that's why I say he is not a true father to the children. I live with my

> mother, he don't know where I am now. I don't like to be that father.'
>
> - 'When he said he is coming and he doesn't come on time then only 2 hours later he phones and says he can't come. When he lies. He never stops shouting at us. And he is sometimes so selfish and greedy.'

don't always acknowledge that their children are their own, and they frequently fail to participate in their children's lives.'[78] But the authors also note that this is changing. In 2004, a national survey of young people aged from eighteen to thirty-two asked young men and women to rank 'what they considered to be the distinguishing characteristics of adulthood. More than 70 per cent of young South Africans, of all race groups and both genders, ranked aspects of parenthood in their top four defining features – Capable of supporting one's family (72.7 per cent); Capable of keeping one's family safe (72.2 per cent); Capable of running a household (71.8 per cent), and Capable of caring for children (70.1 per cent).'[79] The authors note: 'The results show clearly that parenthood and family are important to young South Africans, and young men are increasingly speaking out about their desire to be good fathers.'[80]

Backlash: fathers' rights groups

There is one more twist to the contradictory tale of active fatherhood. Unfortunately, in some countries in the North, fatherhood has become a litmus test for the men's rights agenda. It begins with divorced fathers feeling upset that the mother was given custody of the children. Some then join what have come to be known as 'fathers' rights groups.

Many of these groups also buy into a more general misogynistic agenda, which says that in fact it is women who are favoured by society and men who are disadvantaged, and blames this state of affairs on 'radical feminists'. Statements in the blogosphere and on Twitter express this belief with more vehemence and often with violence against women (see Chapter 7).

Miranda Kaye and Julia Tolmie note in their research into fathers' rights groups in Australia: 'During our research we were struck by the antipathy expressed by many fathers' rights groups not only towards single motherhood, but also "alternative" family forms, particularly lesbian motherhood.' They found that one such group, Men's Confraternity (which in fact wound up in 2009), argued that: 'women should be forced to be financially reliant on men, and that financial reliance should be linked to being contained within a traditional family unit' and that '[m]en should be given first consideration for custody of the children … [as] this … takes away the last remaining excuse for women not to train for proper employment'.[81]

In the USA, Pam Chamberlain, writing on the Political Research Associates website, notes of the fathers' rights organization Fathers and Families: 'What appears at first glance to be an honest plea for fairness is in fact a backlash movement against changing gender-role norms and family structures – cultural shifts that have been influenced by feminist thought and action.'[82]

Fathers' anger, in particular in countries where they feel there is unfair treatment by the courts when it comes to children of divorcing parents, often focuses on the mothers of their children. In the USA, the debates are around the idea of forced joint custody, which many women's groups – for example, the Michigan branch of the National Organization for Women – say that they oppose because: 'it is unworkable for uncooperative parents; it is dangerous for women and their children who are trying to leave or have left violent husbands/fathers; it ignores the diverse, complicated needs of divorced families; and it is likely to have serious, unintended consequences on child support'. The author points out that: 'Forced joint custody is a top legislative priority of fringe fathers' rights groups nationwide.'[83]

Australian masculinities expert Michael Flood says:

I think there's plenty of reason to think that many fathers' rights groups aren't actually very good for fathers at all. They're not good at helping fathers heal from the profound pain and trauma of divorce and separation. They're not good at helping fathers maintain ongoing and respectful relations with their ex-partners, and all the evidence says that that's a really critical predictor of fathers' involvement with children. And finally, they're not very good at helping fathers maintain parenting roles.[84]

Writer Lynne Segal notes that: 'the contemporary reinforcement of fatherhood is problematic in so far as it can be used to strengthen men's control over women and children, in a society where men are already dominant socially, economically and politically'.[85]

Again, this is complex. Support for gender equality and for feminism is by no means a straight-down-the-line divide between the sexes. Women are also involved in the fathers' rights movement. In the USA, Jocelyn Elise Crowley, a specialist in fathers' rights groups, interviewed twenty-three such women, and found that: 'mixed-gender, antifeminist activism has the potential to produce high levels of tension for female participants between their various social identities and their collective movement identity'.[86]

'So scared I was shaking': the way forward in supporting fathers

Being an active father is still something with far fewer traditions, role models and support than being a mother. An internet search for the word 'father' turns up pages of details on Father's Day but not much else. A similar search for 'mother' produces a wide range of articles, stories, images and advertisements. It is not surprising perhaps that in a Pew survey in the USA 73 per cent of mothers said they thought they were doing an 'excellent' or 'very good' job compared with 64 per cent of fathers. Fathers also tended to say that they did not spend enough time with their children, which led to lower ratings of themselves as parents.[87] Says Seani B in the UK: 'I remember when Marcel was born I was so scared I was shaking. I didn't know how to cope. Lots of young dads say they'd welcome some practical advice and support, but there isn't much out there.'[88] Fathers like Seani B are dealing not only with a lack of role models or training, but with race and class. In South Africa, fathers have to deal with a long history of racism which infantilized black men,[89] as well as high levels of unemployment.

But there are a growing number of fathers' organizations, mostly local and small-scale, that recognize this need and are explicitly committed to gender equality. For example, Young Dads TV opposite, and there are many such groups. Many are formed on a self-help basis – and many began when women involved with women's rights groups asked the organizations who were helping them to help their male partners as well.

'Daddy, I love you': Young Dads TV

Young Dads TV is an online service for young fathers in the UK that was set up because a group of young fathers decided it was very difficult to find information about how to be a good father. It is a space for young fathers to share ideas, make films and get involved in their children's lives. There is an interactive map, and a mentoring scheme. Young Dads TV is run by a group of nine fathers who make up the Council of Young Dads. Fathers like James: 'Hello, I'm James. I am 19 and my daughter is two and I am on the Council of Young Dads. The best day about being a dad was about my daughter looking up at me and saying: "Daddy, I love you". It makes my heart melt ... I've got no words for it really.'[90]

In the global South, there are also some groups that work with men in this way, usually funded as part of a development project that focuses on gender, or health, rather than on attitudinal change or direct support for fathers.

MenCare,[91] a global campaign to promote men's caregiving, aimed to challenge this. It was founded in 2012 by Instituto Promundo and Sonke Gender Justice and aimed to spread to ten countries by 2015. It shows the level of interest in the topic that by the end of 2013 it had already brought together partners from twenty-five countries. Among these, for example, are the Fatherhood Support Programme in Turkey run by ACEV, the Mother Child Education Foundation,[92] which aims 'to contribute towards the holistic development of children by addressing the parenting skills and attitudes of their fathers'. Originally developed at the request of mothers, it focuses on raising awareness of child development, fathers' own experiences of being fathered, positive discipline, the importance of play and improving communication within families. Fathers who took part in an evaluation said they spent more time with their children, shouted less and used less harsh discipline, and, according to the mothers, became more involved in parenting and in housework.[93]

In Niger, where maternal and child death rates are high, the Écoles des Maris (Schools for Husbands) aim to transform the attitudes and behaviour of whole communities by training *maris modèles* (model husbands) to learn about, and tell others about, the benefits of using local health services. The men involved, and pregnant women and new mothers, say that the project has changed attitudes towards healthcare and also increased the number of women who give birth with skilled birth attendants.[94]

In Peru, 'Proyecto Papa en Accion' (the Fathers in Action Project) worked with fathers to involve them in early childhood care. As with the ACEV project, the driver was mothers wanting their partners to be more involved in childcare. The fathers' workshops included positive parenting, the importance of reading to children, support sessions for fathers who were having a difficult time adjusting to their caring role, and a session that included the importance of visual and verbal stimulation for early childhood development. After the workshops, fathers said they felt more involved in the family and more connected to their children, that they respected their partners more, used less violence and shared the domestic and caregiving roles more equally.[95]

In India, Instituto Promundo and World Vision India, on

the potential of engaging fathers to end child marriage, found that:

- Women said that fathers' attitudes must be changed – fathers must be sensitized to the importance of education and the health implications of early marriage.
- Issues such as alcoholism, violence against women, children, and gambling were connected with men's feelings of dis-empowerment – of 'not feeling like men' because they were un- or underemployed.
- Young women reported that fathers' increased involvement in caregiving would 'bring more love into the family' and relieve the burden on the shoulders of women and girls.[96]

Juan Antonio, a young father in Mexico, had this advice for other fathers: 'Get involved. I know all that a woman does, as a man it's a little more difficult, but, yes, you can do it. Involve yourself and tell people there is nothing wrong with what you're doing. I mean, try to get involved anywhere.'[97]

In terms of parenting, what seems clear is that women have changed a lot, and men are changing a little. Research from the World Health Organization notes that:

> women are more likely to make long-term, radical changes in their professional lives as a result of having children which, generally, involve working part-time or by changing assignments to better cope with the needs of children and the demands of family life. Men, in contrast, often maintain their full-time employment, take parental leave only for short periods of time and opt for temporary cash benefits; they concentrate instead on short-term efforts to resolve the conflicting demands that arise between work and family life.[98]

In this chapter, perhaps it is as well to leave the last word to a man, for it is here in particular that men need to push the boat out if they want to be equally involved in their children's lives. Gideon Burrows again: 'Today, to be a good dad should mean doing a fairer share of the baby work. Not just the high-profile nappy changes and the bedtime story reading, but an equal share of the slog and the career sacrifice mothers put up with. If the new fatherhood myth is ever to become reality, all those men who claim they would love to work less and spend more time with their children have to stop making excuses. They have to do something about it.'[99]

The next chapter looks at one of the most intractable issues in relationships between men and women – and that is violence.

7 | PROVING THEIR MANHOOD: MEN AND VIOLENCE

The final say

Pascal Akimana was a violent man. And it wasn't until much later in his life that he realized why:

As a child I asked myself why my father continued to fight with my mother every day. I could not get the answer. Then I found out that my father was cheating on my mother; that was the main cause of the fighting. Later I realized that women in the entire village were experiencing gender-based and sexual violence.

To my father, beating and assaulting my lovely mother was the way of proving his manhood. He used to say every day that he was the man; all decisions should be directed to him and he would have the final say.

All this beating that my father was doing to her, many times he would kick her against the wall or beat her with sharp objects. He would insult her in front of us, telling her that she was less than a woman; she was nothing, stupid, ugly, she didn't know how to cook.

It affected me a lot because when he started beating my mother he would turn to me and my sisters, beating us, chasing us away, saying that we are ugly like my mother, stupid, nothing.

Pascal, from Burundi, goes on to explain how the violence he had witnessed made him an angry boy who often got into fights and went on to beat his own girlfriend.

But eventually, he said:

It was because I experienced all this violence and abuse in my family, in my community and in my whole country that I decided to work on advocating for women's rights. Whenever I hear or see an abused woman I remember what my mother and I went through. It is for this reason that I have no regret or doubt about advancing human rights, embracing gender equality, promoting healthy relationships and continuing to strive to end sexual and gender-based violence in my community, society and the entire continent.[1]

Pascal is living proof that violent men can change. As in Pascal's case, the reasons many men are violent have to do with the way they have been socialized and the violence they witnessed or experienced when young. Of course violence needs to be punished, but men also need to have the opportunities to explore the reasons why they behaved in the way that they did. As Gary Barker, masculinities expert, says: 'It is when we reach out with two hands, one that serves as a kind of social control and the other that is supportive, that we are most likely to be successful.'[2]

I spoke to Tapiwa,[3] a male counsellor for Mosaic, an organization in Cape Town, South Africa, that works with both men and women on violence, agrees that reaching out is key: 'Abusive men may learn from their father that violence is the only way to solve a problem. They don't think of themselves as abusers.' He notes that there are barriers to be overcome: 'For men if you ask for counselling you are seen as weak. People judge you. They say "If you are so strong why are you going for counselling? It takes guts for a man to understand he has a problem. It is never easy."'[4]

Peace Ruzage, CEO of Aspire Rwanda, a Kigali-based non-governmental organization providing free vocational skills to vulnerable women, says: 'The problem of violence against women in Rwanda, as with many African countries, is rooted in the cultural beliefs and notions of masculinity reinforced through generations.'[5]

This chapter reveals the high levels of violence against women by men and asks: why does it continue? It examines the link with traditional forms of masculinity, and the cultural and social norms that support and promote men's violence; violence that is socially constructed and about gender relations, internalized gender norms and men's contradictory experiences of power. It looks at some of the reasons why men are violent – and why many are not. It talks about male violence against men and why some feminists find the issue of male rape so difficult. And finally, it examines men's campaigns against violence and asks: what works?

Breaking boundaries not bones

There is something strange about the two eyes behind the black burqa. Despite the immaculate make-up and the steady stare of the brown eyes, the left one looks different from the right. It takes a while to realize that this is because it is surrounded by an enormous dark bruise.

The photo, however, is breaking boundaries rather than bones; it is the first poster against domestic violence in a country where women's rights remain as hidden as the woman's face in the photo: Saudi Arabia.

The text of the poster, part of a campaign by the King Khalid Foundation, says: 'some things can't be covered ... The phenomenon of battered women in Saudi Arabia is much greater than is apparent on the surface ... [it] is a phenomenon found in the dark.'[6]

If the issue of intimate partner violence is beginning to emerge from that darkness even in Saudi Arabia, where women still cannot vote, or even go out in public unless fully covered with only their face showing and accompanied by a man, then maybe even in this difficult arena change is possible.

It is certainly needed. In the online survey for this report, the majority of respondents (61 per cent) felt that violence was the main area where gender equality had deteriorated over the past ten years. In another survey in 2011 by the Association of Women in Development (AWID), women's organizations put ending violence against women as their top priority.[7]

The statistics show that there is a clear and urgent need for action. Violence against women by men continues to be global and shockingly common.[8] According to a 2013 report by the World Health Organization, which analysed data from 141 studies in 81 countries, 35 per cent of women around the world have been raped or physically abused, the majority (80 per cent) by a partner or spouse.[9]

- In the USA, the National Network to End Domestic Violence reports that three women die each day because of domestic violence. One woman in four experiences domestic violence in her lifetime.[10]
- A research study on domestic violence against women in five states in India found that 84 per cent of the 1,250 respondents had experienced physical violence in one form or another.[11]
- Interviews with 42,000 women across Europe found that more than one in five has experienced physical and/or sexual violence from either a current or previous partner.[12]

- In Vietnam, 58 per cent of women who had been married reported having experienced at least one type of physical, sexual or emotional violence.[13]
- In Ecuador, the 2011 National Survey on Family Relationships and Gender-based Violence against Women found that 60.6 per cent of the women interviewed had suffered some type of gender violence: physical, psychological, sexual or financial.

The prevalence of violence against women, and the fact that it cuts across class, age, religion, marital status, sexual orientation, race and ethnic origin, indicates that it is not only common, but that it is still seen as acceptable. Many definitions of violence include physical and sexual violence, but also psychological and economic violence. It seems that it takes very little to trigger this violence, as the Twitter abuse against Caroline Criado Perez in the UK shows, threatened with rape just for the suggestion that writer Jane Austen should feature on British banknotes.[14] Two of her abusers have now been jailed – the fact that one was a woman shows just how entrenched negative views of women are in both sexes – but the others have never been found. The boundaries of what is seen as 'acceptable' seem to be constantly pushed back.

In the UK, Laura Bates launched 'Everyday Sexism'[15] in 2012, asking women to send in their stories. By 2013, she had had more than 25,000 responses from fifteen countries. The stories came from girls and women from all classes and ethnicities. They are shocking evidence that sexism and misogyny remain as rife as ever.

- A girl in Pakistan described hiding sexual abuse for the sake of 'family honour'.
- A woman in Brazil was harassed by three men who tried to drag her into their car when she ignored them.

- In Germany, a woman had her crotch and bottom groped so frequently she described it as 'the norm'.
- In Mexico, a university student was told by her professor: '*Calladita te ves mas bonita*' (you look prettier when you shut up).
- In Israel, a teacher with a master's degree who speaks six languages was told: 'I wasn't a good enough homemaker for my future husband.'
- In France, a man exposed himself to twelve- and sixteen-year-old sisters as they tried to picnic in a public park.
- On a bus in India, a woman was too afraid to report the man pressing his erect penis into her back.[16]

In India, 'eve-teasing' is a commonly used term to embrace behaviour which ranges from verbal abuse to groping. It is a serious problem for women, and a number of campaigns, including online campaigns, have been set up to combat it. One of these was in Bangalore, where a supporter noted: 'If we, as a society, really want to deal with this issue, then the solution is not to teach women and girls how to build their lives around avoiding situations that lead to eve-teasing, but to teach young boys and men the correct way to treat women and express their liking and respect for them.'[17]

The problem with violence against women, particularly in the home, is that often it is still seen as a private matter between a woman and a man (the issue of lesbian, gay and transgender violence is pretty well ignored). So although international and national laws prohibit domestic violence, it is still rare for men to be prosecuted.

For example, rape in marriage was made illegal in many countries only quite recently. In many countries, women as well as men are socialized to see wife-beating as a 'normal' part of a marital relationship. For example, in Nicaragua, research found that 25 per cent of rural and 15 per cent of urban women said a husband was justified in beating his wife for neglecting the children or the house.[18] In Egypt, between 40 and 81 per cent of women said beatings were justified for reasons that included neglecting the house or children, refusing sex, answering back or disobedience.[19] In Vietnam, 35.8 per cent of women say they accept violent treatment from their husbands in certain situations.[20]

And it cannot be assumed that attitudes are necessarily improving down the generations. For example, in Scotland a study found that 50 per cent of boys and 33 per cent of girls said that

---

Examples of social and cultural norms that promote violence against women[21]

- A man has a right to assert power over a woman and is considered socially superior – e.g. India, Nigeria and Ghana
- A man has a right to physically discipline a woman for 'incorrect' behaviour – e.g. India, Nigeria and China
- Physical violence is an acceptable way to resolve conflict in a relationship – e.g. USA
- Intimate partner violence is a 'taboo' subject – e.g. South Africa
- Divorce is shameful – e.g. Pakistan
- Sex is a man's right in marriage – e.g. Pakistan
- Sexual activity (including rape) is a marker of masculinity – e.g. South Africa
- Girls are responsible for controlling a man's sexual urges.

under certain circumstances it was acceptable for a man to hit a woman or force her to have sex, and 36 per cent of boys said this was something they might do themselves.[22] In South Africa, the incidence of rape continues to increase – one study found that 27.6 per cent of the men interviewed said they had raped a woman.[23]

Mnestisi belongs to Imbizo Yamododa or Gathering of Men, launched in 2012 by Comacare, which works with young men with brain injury.[24] Although only in his twenties himself, Mnestisi told me he thinks violence has increased since his childhood: 'When I was young it was there but it is much worse now – they are using pangas [machetes]. When we were growing up we would

---

The abusive husband who became a role model[25]

Hassan Shyaka, 45, can barely read or write. But the cassava farmer from Nyarugenge district in Kigali province never leaves home without his blue pen neatly clipped to his shirt pocket. Remembering the past, Shyaka cannot believe how a simple decision catapulted him into the most respected position in the village.

'Not beating my wife changed my life,' Shyaka laughs. 'I was the most notorious man in the village – so notorious for being foul-mouthed and violent to Hasina that women used to hate me,' he admits. Beside him 42-year-old Hasina Nyiraminani, his wife of 22 years, nods.

Shyaka confesses he used to beat Nyiraminani whenever she confronted him about the rumours of his illegal 'second marriage'. In 2011, after his children witnessed him leave her seriously wounded, the community leader

fight over girls but it was not really serious – it would fade away. Now it is like watching a horror movie. They carry knives, people do mob justice because the police are useless. People can't even travel to another area because of gangsterism.'[26]

Other influences include the media, and in particular exposure, often at a young age, to violent pornography on the internet which demeans and degrades women. We saw in Chapter 3 the effects of pornography on relationships between young women and men. It is clear that millions of young people today are exposed to violent images via television, films and the internet, often from an early age. In the USA, the average young person between eight and eighteen years old watches around 10,000

---

referred him to Rwanda Men's Resource Centre's RWAM-REC gender workshop.

'The workshop forced me to rethink my relationship with my family, and whether I was a role model to my children. It shamed me,' says Shyaka.

According to Nyiraminani, he returned a 'reformed' man. No beating, no shouting – Shyaka left everyone shocked. Before long, he was being asked to counsel and share his experience to help save other marriages.

Last year, to his surprise, he was chosen to be a community leader. 'Today I tell everyone to respect their wife if they want to change their life,' Shyaka swells with pride.

Adapted from an article written by Nishtha Chugh, one of the winners of the Guardian's *International Development Journalism Competition 2013.*

violent acts every year on television.[27] Ninety per cent of these have images of women being beaten, raped or killed. There are still many debates as to how much this translates into actual violence. But in one survey by Men Can Stop Rape, respondents were asked: Do violent video games that blur the line between fantasy and reality support violence against women and girls? Of 963 respondents, 50 per cent said yes, 31 per cent said no.[28]

Most of the violence against women is perpetrated by men. It seems to be a recent trend to point out that women can also be violent, as if this balances out the equation. Of course women can be violent too, but in general they are less physically strong than men, and, as we will see later in this chapter, do not have the same drive to be violent in order to prove themselves. For men the link between violence and masculinity is part of their contradictory experiences of power.

The statistics bear this out: in the USA, for example, women perpetrate sexual abuse against boys in 14 per cent of cases and against girls in 6 per cent of cases.[29] In the UK, women accounted for 7 per cent of all convictions for domestic violence in 2011, according to the government's Crown Prosecution Service.[30] In addition, studies have shown that women who are violent to-wards their partners commonly report using violence to defend themselves.[31] For example, in one sample 75 per cent of women who said they had been violent said it was in self-defence.[32] And another study noted: 'It is very unlikely that women's aggression will end unless their partners' violence against them is stopped.'[33]

Legislation should be one way of stopping violence. And there has been progress. Laws against gender-based violence exist at international level and in most countries and continue to be updated and improved. For example, Brazil's Maria da Penha Law on Violence against Women (2006), the result of long campaigns by women's organizations, provides a variety of legal protections, including special courts, preventive detentions for severe threats, increased penalties for perpetrators, and affirmative measures to assist women and to educate the public. The government of Brazil also put resources into implementation – in August 2007, the president of Brazil announced a budget of US$590 million for this purpose.[34]

But all too often laws against violence against women are not enforced and men are never punished. Danijela Pesic, from the Autonomous Women's Centre, in Belgrade, Serbia, which has worked on violence against women for the past two decades, says that only by improving the enforcement of legislation already in place can there be systematic solutions for victims.[35] Women also need to be able to report violence – often they are too afraid. A Europe-wide survey found that only 14 per cent of women reported their most serious incident of intimate partner violence to the police.[36]

'Whatever the complex social and psychological causes of men's violence, it wouldn't continue if there weren't explicit or tacit permission in social customs, legal codes, law enforcement, and certain religious teachings,' says Michael Kaufman, co-founder of the White Ribbon campaign of men against violence against women.[37] There may be international laws, and laws in most countries, against violence and against violence against women, but they are generally disregarded because they go against the norm that violence is acceptable – or even expected – behaviour for men.

'Guys who fight are seen as cool'

The root cause of men's violence is the way they are brought up to see violence – both against women and against other men – as intrinsic to being a man. In fact, what is surprising is not that so many men are violent, but that most are not, because violence is such an integral part of the construction of masculinities and of patriarchy. 'For the most part, the world doesn't make gender equitable men – it spends a lot of time making men who are angry and disconnected and violent,' says Gary Barker, International Director of Instituto Promundo.[38]

In Chapter 3 we looked at the 'missing women' in many countries, the result of sex-selective abortion and infanticide of girls relating to their status as second-class citizens. But it is also possible to count the 'missing men'. As with girls, this varies hugely both between and within countries. In Brazil, high rates of homicide among men mean that there were 4 million 'missing men' in 2012. And lower life expectancies almost everywhere for men mean that there are far more older women than there are older men.

Melanie Judge, South African activist and social commentator, notes in her blog:[39]

> Masculinity is achieved through gender violence. Certain forms of 'manliness' are predicated on men's violent use of power over women and against those men perceived as weak or 'unmanly'. This assertion of 'manhood', which is perceived as normal or natural, kills women ...
>
> Gender violence works as a strategy of discipline and control over persons' lives and bodies. It systematically ensures compliance with strict gender and sexual codes. It is employed by all of us, and against all of us. It defines what 'real men' and 'real women' should be and what happens to them if they're not ...

Danijela Pesic from the Autonomous Women's Centre in Serbia says: 'The main cause of domestic violence is patriarchal values. Men have to stop believing they can be violent, and for this to happen we need to change our perception of gender roles, starting as early as kindergarten.'[40] Lori Heise, senior lecturer at the London School of Hygiene and Tropical Medicine (LSHTM) and chief executive of STRIVE, an international research consortium dedicated to studying the structural drivers of HIV, notes: 'The more I work on violence against women, the more I become convinced that the real way forward is to redefine what it means to be male.'[41] 'The problem of violence against women in Rwanda, as with many African countries, is rooted in the cultural beliefs and notions of masculinity reinforced through generations,' says Peace Ruzage, CEO of Aspire Rwanda.[42]

Bearing in mind this underlying norm that male anger and violence are seen as socially acceptable, part of the theme of 'being tough' that we have seen in attitudes to masculinity, there are a number of factors that are likely to lead to male violence, whether it be against women or against other men. One study with young men in the Balkans identified seven key causes of violence, one of which was precisely this – 'expectations of being a man'. The pressure from others, especially their peers, to 'prove themselves' as men is extremely strong. The research found that 'most young men see physical fighting as unavoidable for a man'; and that it shaped what it meant to be a man: 'You cannot grow up to be a man without fighting.'[43]

Syaldi Sahude of the Alliance for the New Man in Indonesia, which organizes social media campaigns and discussions among male university students, told me: 'Many men don't understand how to express their feelings so they do it with anger.'[44]

Research in the USA and South Africa found that young men who adhered to traditional views of manhood were more likely to engage in substance use, violence and delinquency and unsafe sexual practices.[45] The IMAGES research in ten countries also found this consistently.[46]

The Balkans research identified seven main causes of male violence, all of which have their roots in the same patriarchal attitudes:

1   Exposure to family violence – 'If you are raised well in family you will not behave violently'.
2   Exposure to media violence.
3   Individual feelings of inadequacy – 'He's unwanted in a group and all groups reject and insult him. One day he'll definitely be violent.'
4   Sexual jealousy, and related feelings of insecurity – 'Jealousy leads to fear, which leads to powerlessness, which leads to [rage which leads to] violence.'
5   Stress related to economic insecurity and jobs – 'Unemployment raises frustration which makes tension into the family, and this transfers on kids who then are more likely to be violent.'
6   Alcohol and drugs as a catalyst – 'alcohol makes it possible to beat someone'.
7   Expectations of being a man.[47]

From an early age, boys and young men are taught to believe that violence is a sign of strength. The World Health Organization study on violence found that boys are two to three times more likely than girls to have been in a physical fight.[48] As bell hooks writes: 'there is only one emotion that patriarchy values when expressed by men: that emotion is anger. Real men get mad.'[49] A young man in the Balkans said: 'Physical strength brings respect,' and another noted: 'guys who always fight are seen as cool'.[50]

'If you are raised well you will not behave violently'

Studies have found that witnessing or being subject to violence as a child – whether at home, at school or in the street – often leads to a continuing cycle of male violence down the generations.[51] And in some countries and cultures, this is a common occurrence – research in Peru found that 'out of 100 caregivers, 10.9 per cent said they were assaulted by their partner when the latter was intoxicated and 11.8 per cent of household respondents reported that one of the partners in the home got drunk at least once a week'. Research in 2009 for a paper on violence found that 'all the children interviewed reported having heard or witnessed cases of domestic violence in their own families'.[52] In school, boys were more likely to be beaten than girls.

'Boys who are subjected to harsh physical punishment, who are physically abused themselves, or who witness their mothers being beaten are more likely to abuse their partners later in life,' says Lori Heise from the STRIVE research consortium.[53] Boys who see their fathers and other men being violent towards women come to think that this is normal behaviour, and when they become fathers are likely to continue to use violence towards family members.

In the online survey for this report, respondents were asked: 'What factors prevent men becoming involved in gender equality?'; 87.5 per cent said: 'Strong religious and cultural norms to adhere to traditional masculinities', 82.2 per cent said 'family attitudes/upbringing' and 'fear of not being seen as a "real man" by other men'.

A study in six countries by the International Center for Research on Women (ICRW) and the MenEngage Alliance found that the most significant factor for men who were violent at home was that they had been victims of violence when they were children, either abused and beaten themselves, or witnessing the abuse of their mother.[54] UNICEF notes that boys who saw their fathers use violence against their mothers 'are twice as likely to become abusive men as are the sons of non-violent parents'.[55] Research in Uganda and Nigeria found that young men saw violence against women as an acceptable extension of male violence at home.[56]

But, as the STRIVE study notes: 'The pattern is not inevitable, however, and a key question for future research is what genetic, situational, socio-cultural, and life-course factors distinguish those who later become violent from those who go on to form healthy relationships?'[57] Sometimes boys who have experienced violence at home consciously refuse to be violent themselves: 'I don't agree that a man should beat his wife ... I've seen my father slap my mother,' said one young man from the Balkans.[58]

Unemployment, alcohol and violence

While patriarchy and traditional attitudes towards being a man may be the main cause of male violence, there are other factors that may be secondary contributors. For example, in many parts of the world men (and women) still see the man's main role as the provider for the family. Even in countries where men and women both undertake paid work (see Chapter 5) it was only one or two generations ago that traditional middle-class families had a mother at home and a father who went out to work. The roots of the provider role run deep. So when men no longer have that role, they may feel useless and frustrated, and take this frustration out on those closest to them in the only way they know how – violence. This is not to condone such violence, but to try to explain it. Gary Barker, International Director of Instituto Promundo, notes:

If work is an imperative to achieve a socially recognised version of manhood, the syllogism is that no work means no manhood. It means that women will not find you attractive as long-term partners. It means the police will harass you. It means your parents will hound you to find work. As a result, some young men turn to other ways to achieve respect or recognition – ranging from gangs to domestic violence and substance use.[59]

The IMAGES study of men in five countries, conducted by the International Center for Research on Women and Instituto Promundo, found that work-related or economic stress had negative effects on men, including depression, ideas of suicide, arrests and use of violence.[60]

A man in Vietnam, who was taking part in a Responsible Men's

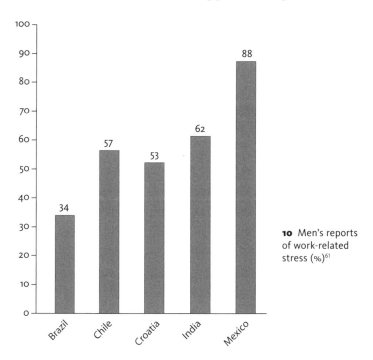

10 Men's reports of work-related stress (%)[61]

Club, a project for men who were violent towards their wives, said: 'To be honest with you, I made violence also because of the economic situation. I had to be at home so I felt depressed. They [men] went for work and I had to be at home. I felt depressed and once you are depressed you easily make violence in the family ... As a man I like to be the pillar in the house. ... As a husband, I should never be dependent [on my wife].'[62]

In the current economic crisis, young men in particular may use violence as a way of expressing their frustration in the face of continuing unemployment.[63] A study by Oxfam GB on the effects of the global economic crisis found that in South-East Asia focus group discussions revealed an increase in already high levels of domestic violence. These union officials in Indonesia told the story of Nuning, who 'worked in a garment factory in North Jakarta and her wage supported her extended family as her husband was unemployed. When she was laid off, he got very angry and started to beat her. In this case our union tried to mediate by meeting with the family and explaining that the dismissal was the impact of the crisis, not the fault of the wife and that the violence had to stop. We are hearing many cases like this.'[64]

Alcohol and drugs are also key factors that instigate or exacerbate men's violence. The World Health Organization notes that: 'Drunkenness is an important immediate situational factor that can precipitate violence. In a Swedish study, about three-quarters of violent offenders and around half the victims of violence were intoxicated at the time of the incident, and in the Cambridge study, many of the boys fought after drinking.'[65] The STRIVE research found: 'Excessive drinking by men has been strongly associated with partner violence in nearly every setting that has been studied.'[66] The IMAGES study in six countries found that: 'Alcohol abuse was also shown to be associated with Intimate

Male rape: a feminist issue

Perhaps one of the most under-reported issues in terms of male violence is the rape of men by other men. But it is also an interesting case study in the way in which the women's and men's rights agendas are portrayed as conflictual.

Very little research has been done in this area, perhaps because being raped is such a source of shame that few male victims actually come forward. So statistics are hard to find. In the USA, the Pennsylvania Coalition Against Rape says that one out of every thirty-three men has been the victim of attempted or completed rape.[67] In times of conflict, very few rape services cater for men. 'The risks of revealing trauma without any concrete structures in place to help survivors recover may outweigh any emotional benefit from reporting trauma that then goes unrecognised by NGOs and other organisations, re-traumatising male survivors and reifying the idea that men cannot be victims,' says Emily Cody, programme officer for the African Centre for Justice and Peace Studies in Uganda. Although in theory legislation against gender-based violence should also apply to men, there are very few laws that will protect men as well as women – the UN changed its definition of rape to cover male victims only in 2011.[68]

Those campaigning to gain recognition for male rape frequently blame women – particularly feminists – for the fact that it is not on the agenda either internationally or in national and local non-governmental organizations. A paper by the Refugee Law Project in Uganda notes:

One argument by many feminists is that women are the 'vast majority' of victims, and that women and girls are 'disproportionately affected' by sexual violence. Although such claims are rarely accompanied by supporting data, the argument continues that because women form the 'vast majority' of victims, finite resources should be focused on women. This reasoning has obstructed both the acknowledgment of male victims and the provision of aid to such victims.[69]

There seems to be even less data on male rape, and what exists is mainly from conflict situations. But it indicates that it is much more common than previously believed. For example, the Refugee Law Project paper[70] quotes: '76 per cent of male political prisoners surveyed in one prison in El Salvador in 1986, described at least one incidence of sexual torture.'[71] In eastern Europe, a study of 6,000 survivors of detention camps in the former Yugoslavia found that 80 per cent of men reported having been raped.[72] From 2003 to 2004, investigators documented sexual abuse of Iraqi detainees at Abu Ghraib prison in Iraq by US soldiers.[73] Women's organizations do not deny that male rape is a problem, but believe that it is on a far smaller scale than female rape. Once again, the debates are often about resources, with campaigners for male rape saying that there is no funding for male victims, and women's rights campaigners not wanting to lose any of the increasingly small amounts of money that they have access to, especially in a financial climate where rape crisis centres are struggling.[74]

However, the controversy does not help women or men. Stereotypes that portray women as victims and men as perpetrators serve neither sex well. As Melanie Judge, South African social commentator and activist, told me: 'It is important to look at the rape of men. It speaks to the system of masculinities that says only weak men get raped. Male rape is keeping masculinities in place – it is a feminist issue.'[75]

Partner Violence (IPV). In all research sites, men who regularly (at least monthly) have five or more drinks at one time report higher levels of IPV compared to men who do not report this heavy drinking.'[76]

In 2011, in Scotland, police reported that domestic abuse rose by 138.8 per cent when a soccer game between traditional rivals Celtic and Ranger was played on a Saturday, with smaller but still significant rises (96.6 per cent and 56.8 per cent) for games played on Sundays and weekday evenings.[77] Men whose teams lose are likely to go out and drink, and come home and beat their wives.

Male hierarchies: men killing men

It is sometimes forgotten that gender-based violence (as opposed to violence against women) is also about men killing other men as well as killing women. Melanie Judge again: 'The hierarchies that exist between men require violence to be maintained and so men too are its victims.'[78]

Men kill more men than they kill women, although more men are killed by strangers and more women are killed by intimate partners. In the USA, based on data from 1980 and 2008, men represented 77 per cent of homicide victims and nearly 90 per cent of offenders.[79] Homicide rates for young men in particular are very high: the World Health Organization estimates that if you are a young man between the ages of fifteen and twenty-nine in the Americas, the risk of dying from homicide is almost twenty-eight times great than the average risk worldwide.[80]

In Brazil, the 2000 census found that there were nearly 200,000 fewer men than women aged between fifteen and twenty-nine because of higher rates of mortality from gun-related violence.[81] Once again, it is low-income young men who suffer the most, and young black men in particular. Tatiana Moura, Jose Luis Ratton and Gary Barker from Instituto Promundo point out that homicide rates have come down in Brazil, but not for this segment of the population. The authors link this clearly back to the promotion of a kind of masculinity embedded in violence, social exclusion and racism: 'There is a hyper-masculine culture deeply rooted in the police force, drug gangs, the media and the general population in Brazil. Violence by police is tolerated, violence in the media is tolerated, violence at football matches is tolerated, violence by parents is tolerated and violence against indigenous groups is tolerated. The connection between violence and manhood in Brazil must be severed.'[82]

This is not just a problem for young black men in Brazil, but for everyone: there seems to be a clear link between using violence in the street and using it at home. In the IMAGES study, 'men who owned firearms or carried out other violence or criminal behaviour were also more likely to report having used intimate partner violence'.[83] In the USA, a woman is 270 per cent more likely to die from being murdered if there is a gun in the house.[84] Ironically, she may have purchased the gun in order to protect herself from attack.

Fear among the *maras*

El Salvador has one of the highest murder rates in the world. Up to ten people die every day in this tiny country. The majority are young men who become involved in gangs, known as *maras* or *pandillas*.

Cindy Romero, who is an elected youth councillor in Ciudad Arce, one of the twenty most violent towns in the country, says: 'In this municipality there are places that are fully controlled by gangs and where even the police don't go.' The *maras* are known for their brutality. Murders, rapes and beheadings are common – in August 2010 a six-year-old girl was beheaded on her way to school.

Most Salvadoreans will tell you that the gang violence comes from the United States: 1.1 million El Salvadoreans emigrated to the United States in 2010, making up 2.7 per cent of the USA's total foreign-born population. El Salvador itself has an estimated 6.7 million population – thus the impact of emigration to the USA must be strongly felt. Many become involved in gangs there and bring a gang culture, driven by drugs and extortion, back with them when they return. The violence can also be traced to the number of guns in the country and to the history of extreme violence during more than a decade of civil war in the 1980s. Add poverty and youth unemployment into the mix and it makes an explosive cocktail.

Whatever its origins, the power of the *maras* lies not only in their physical presence, but in the fear that they spread. Javier, aged twenty, from Cabanas, another violent city, says: 'We are the second-most violent country in Latin America and in most cases it is boys that are affected – violence against young men is higher than violence against young women. We face pressure from the police and the authorities – the police search us and harass us just because we are young and male.' His view is confirmed in a study which found that victims as well as perpetrators of homicide were mostly young men, and that in 2004 ten men were killed for every woman. The same report notes that: 'this data confirms the idea that youth are usually the victims of violence, rather than the victimisers'.

There is a link between the violence in the streets and violence in the family. One study of El Salvador's gangs found that almost eight out of every ten gang members came from a violent home. Carla, aged eighteen, says: 'The first education we receive is from our parents. If our parents are not violent in the home we are not going to be violent outside.'

Some young people talk about witnessing parents abusing their children. Seventeen-year-old Nelson says: 'In my neighbourhood there is a kid who sells vegetables and if he doesn't sell them he gets hit. Last year the police came to talk to them because neighbours called the police. But they didn't take the kid away and nothing happened.'

The government is trying to crack down on the gangs. Prisons are packed, there is a poster campaign against violence and, in September 2010, it introduced a law to criminalize the *maras*. In response, the *maras* brought the capital, San Salvador, to a halt for three days by forcing transport to shut down; 80 per cent of public buses stopped running and many businesses closed as well. Nonetheless, the law was passed. Among other things, it put in place measures to prevent young people becoming involved in crime. The young people themselves believe that active participation and education can help to prevent future generations becoming violent. Cindy, aged twenty, says: 'Violence is a wide topic because it is where all rights are taken away. We have to be honest and say that most families are not able to educate their kids about violence – it is passed on from generation to generation.' Hector, also aged twenty, said that he thought it was important to work with young people because they were still at the stage when their identities were being formed and there was the possibility of changing their behaviour. In addition: 'If young people lead other young people then they are more likely to get motivated.' In the meantime, the metal grilles remain on people's homes and the gangs continue to roam freely in many parts of the country.[85]

'She provoked me': blaming women

It is still very common for men – and women – to blame the women who are the victims of violence. In the UK, a survey for Amnesty International found that more than one in four respondents thought a woman was partially or totally responsible for being raped if she was wearing sexy or revealing clothing, and more than one in five held the same view if a woman had had many sexual partners.[86]

In Peru, this man involved in a programme for male perpetrators of violence against their partners said: 'She provoked me, we have disagreements about decisions that I make, she tells me I am a fool and compares me with others. It irritates me, makes me feel like I've failed as a man and that makes me feel ashamed, that angers me, she knows how I get but likes to provoke me and that is why it is her fault that I shout and hit her.'[87]

In India, research with young men in 2011 found that many still believed women fell into two categories: those who were sex objects and those eligible for marriage. If a young woman agreed to an assignation, they were expected to have sex. Refusal

---

Zaina's story[88]

'I was going to school and a soldier raped me while I was walking there. I was 14 years old. The men were from the Mai [pro-Congolese government militia group in the Democratic Republic of Congo]. I was very scared. I cried out for help but no one came because I was in a forest and no one heard me. Despite my cries, they carried on doing what they were doing to me. It's a habit here. Men in militias or in the military take women by force and no one talks to them about it, and no one stops them. It's commonplace.

'After being raped, my life became unbearable in my family. When I got home I told my family what happened. Directly afterwards they asked me how I could have accepted what had happened to me, and they drove me away.

was a justification for violence.[89] In South Africa, where a rape reputedly occurs every four minutes, a survey of 250,000 male and female youths in school showed that young men believed that: 'girls have no right to refuse sex with their boyfriends; girls mean yes when they say no; girls like sexually violent guys; girls who are raped ask for it; girls enjoy being raped'.[90]

Treating a woman or a girl who has been raped as though she is the guilty one is not unusual. In the United Arab Emirates, Marte Deborah Dalelv, a Norwegian interior designer, reported that she had been raped in July 2013. She was detained and sentenced to sixteen months in prison for having unlawful sex, making a false statement and illegal consumption of alcohol, but was pardoned by what was effectively a royal decree a few

They refused to let me go back to school and they kicked me out. So, I came here to my maternal aunt's house. I do not understand how they could treat me like this.

'There are two of us – my sister and myself. We were both raped. When we eat, we eat separately from the other children. Normally my aunt doesn't mistreat us. But when a member of our immediate family came to her house, she would begin to mistreat us. For instance, when I touched my aunt's things in her house she insulted me. But the community network visited us and gave advice to my aunt. And sometimes they give us cabbage seeds so that helps us with our farming. Except for the community network no-one comes to talk to me or to give me advice. What I want is for my parents to accept me again. That is my main worry.'

days later and released. Her rapist, who was also charged, was also freed as she dropped her case.[91] The fact that women are blamed, imprisoned and ostracized for being the victims of rape underlines the importance of working with men and the wider community on the issue of violence against women.

Addressing the root causes

There is a photo on Indian journalist Mari Marcel Thekaekara's blog[92] about the rape in Delhi in December 2012 of the woman who has come to be known by many as 'Nirbhaya' – 'the one without fear'. It shows a crowd in the darkness of a New Delhi night, each holding a candle to the woman who fought back so bravely against her attackers. What marks it out is not just the numbers and the range of people of all different ages, but the fact that there are significant numbers of men protesting alongside women.

This is not a new phenomenon, but it is perhaps not recognized outside certain circles. There are still relatively few people who are aware of the scale of the violence being committed against women – and even fewer who link it to a masculinities crisis – but there have been a growing number of campaigns in recent years. Perhaps the best known is One Billion Rising, which asks people 'to do one thing in the next year to end violence against women' and has designated 14 February as V-day (after Eve Ensler's *The Vagina Monologues*). Its profile-raising has been hugely successful; in 2013, the campaign claimed a billion people in 207 countries responding to the call with marches, petitions and national and local campaigns.[93] And many of these are men as well as women.

One Billion Rising is pre-dated by the White Ribbon campaign, a movement of men against violence against women, which was founded in Canada in 1991 by Michael Kaufman, Jack Layton and Ron Sluser, and was quickly picked up by other men.[94] White Ribbon has had campaigns in more than seventy countries around the world. It began indirectly as a protest against women dying a violent death at the hands of a man – in this case anti-feminist Marc Lépine, who killed fourteen women in Montreal in 1989.

There are many local and national campaigns in which men have become involved against male violence– for example, One Man Can in South Africa (see box, page 206); the men of strength campaign in the USA;[95] Men Against Violence Against Women (MAVAW) in the USA;[96] Responsible Men's Clubs in Vietnam, which worked with husbands who were perpetrators of violence against their wives. At the end of the sessions, even in a very gender-unequal society, almost 70 per cent of men said they had not behaved violently since they began the work.[97]

But even taking a stand against violence against women is complicated. All too often the only response to an atrocity like the rape in Delhi, or the appalling rape and torture and murder of seventeen-year-old Anene Booysen in South Africa, is to call for the blood of the perpetrators. Of course they must be punished – violence demands an end to impunity – but individual punishment is not enough.

Such appalling acts need to be set in a context that also examines why they happen – and what can be done in terms of changing attitudes and behaviour and looking at the structural drivers of rape and violence. 'Social change is a messy process,' says Jackson Katz, a masculinities expert. 'We need more men with the guts to stand up and say abusive behavior is abusive behaviour, and it's not right, and it doesn't make me less of a man to point that out.'[98]

Janine and Anthony, whose story we heard in Chapter 3, were

involved with Mosaic, an organization in Cape Town that started out working with women who had suffered violence and abuse. So why work with men? Zarina Majiet, from Mosaic, was quite clear about this when I spoke to her: 'Because the women that we work with asked us to. They are victims of violence. But they didn't want their partners or husbands to go to prison. They just wanted the violence to stop. So we started a male counselling programme.'

She continued: 'To be honest, it was also because ninety per cent of the women who come to the rape crisis centres go back to the men who were violent. So we need to address the root cause of the problem as well as help the women who are victims.'[99]

In Indonesia too, the Men Care + programme,[100] which pro-

One Man Can: 'See it and stop it'[101]

South Africa has amongst the highest levels of domestic violence and rape of any country in the world. Research conducted by the Medical Research Council in 2004 shows that every six hours, a woman is killed by her intimate partner. South Africa's National Injury Mortality Surveillance System also tells us that the rate at which South African men kill each other is amongst the highest in the world.

The One Man Can Campaign is run by Sonke Gender Justice in South Africa. It supports men and boys to take action to end domestic and sexual violence and to promote healthy, equitable relationships that men and women can enjoy – passionately, respectfully and fully.

The One Man Can Campaign promotes the idea that

motes men's involvement as fathers, husbands and individuals opposed to violence, is called the 'Laki-laki Peduli: Bekerjasama untuk Kesetaraan' (Men Care: Working Together for Equality) campaign. Sri Kusyuniati is country representative for Rutgers WPF, a Dutch non-governmental organization that funds the work: 'I realized that our [previous] programs [in reducing gender-based violence and maternal mortality rates] had been unsuccessful thus far. After conducting research, which was helped by various institutions including the University of Indonesia's (UI) research center on family issues, we found that we needed a positive approach toward men in order to help reduce the rates. Let's stop blaming men, but rather encourage them to be more caring.'[102] Men also need to challenge other men when they see

---

each one of us has a role to play, that each one of us can create a better, more equitable and more just world. At the same time, the campaign encourages men to work together with other men and with women to take action – to build a movement, to demand justice, to claim our rights and to change the world.

One Man Can believes that young men have a particular responsibility to challenge violence against women and girls. Every day in South Africa young men and women as well as boys and girls face alarmingly high levels of domestic and sexual violence. One Man Can gives young men and women ideas about what they can do to change this. These include 'examining your own beliefs and actions'; 'supporting a survivor'; 'taking action'; and 'See it and stop it'.

violence being done to women. The 'Ring the Bell' project in India does just that. A powerful public service announcement encourages men when they hear another man abusing a woman inside a nearby home to ring the doorbell to interrupt the violence and to show that it is not just a private matter.[103] Pramod Tiwari, a government worker, explained what happened to him:

> In front of my house, there is a family that drags the woman by her hair. They drag her near the gas and say 'burn yourself'. They don't give her food. In winters I see her without warm clothes. In summers she has no fan. She stays locked in a room, like a prisoner. After watching the *Bell Bajao* ads, we started making some noise every time we heard violence. The violence used to stop for the time being. Eventually it stopped entirely. I did feel good about helping her. Earlier I used to feel helpless around her. Now she's happy, so I am happy. It was like helping my own child. I want to thank *Bell Bajao* for inspiring me to take action.[104]

On International Women's Day 2014, Laura Bates of the Everyday Sexism project[105] encouraged followers to share their stories of men standing up against sexism. The tweets showed clearly that there were many men who were standing up against sexism, abuse and discrimination – and for gender equality. One twenty-two-year-old man wrote: 'I cannot stop reading this website ... More and more I find myself calling out men when they make these comments. It isn't easy, and one instance will not change their behaviour. However, I think it does make a difference ... Will encourage other men to stop this behaviour when they see it.' Other tweets included:[106]

- 'My husband always challenges sexism. He doesn't want our daughter experiencing some of the things I have.'

- 'I keep asking "why is that funny?" and: "I don't get it," when guys make sexist jokes. Embarrasses them as they explain it.'
- 'My 12yo son learned to do laundry and cook because he wants his someday-wife "to have respect for me".'
- 'The boy in the park today, who, when his friend started making sexist comments, told him to shut up and stop being a dick.'
- 'My high school teacher took a class to explain the difference of sex and gender, the problems of binarism & stereotyping.'
- 'My brother, who identifies himself as a feminist and who challenges casual sexism and misogyny relentlessly.'
- 'My 18yr-old son who walked out of work placement disgusted by degrading images of women. It meant the world to me.'[107]

Ending men's violence against women – and against other men – means ending impunity and changing social norms. It also involves recognizing just how toxic manhood and boyhood are for boys and men – and how that toxicity turns into violence against women and girls.

This is a challenge that men and women need to take on together in the name of equality – or else the violence will continue from generation to generation as it has for so many hundreds of years. Working together means there is a chance for change. And it needs to be grabbed with both hands before another man kills. A feminist project? Certainly. But also one that affects us all, regardless of gender.

8 | CONCLUSION: BECOMING CONNECTED

Men and the future of feminism

Feminism is back in fashion. Even since I first proposed the idea for this book in 2012, the number of articles in the media, interviews and blogs on the subject have burgeoned. Tweets fly in their thousands, commenting on feminism, reporting sexist behaviour or giving examples of new initiatives. There are hundreds of feminist websites, mostly set up by young women. There have also been discussions and disagreements between feminists[1] – and plenty of abuse from outside the movement.[2]

But men have remained largely peripheral to most of these discussions, despite the small, but growing, involvement of men all over the world in organizing for gender equality or against violence.

This book argues that this needs to change. Unless men become central to discussions about gender rather than being marginalized, they will continue to be a block to the achievement of gender equality. This does not mean that women lose the space or the resources that they need for their own work, but simply that the doors remain open for dialogue and sometimes for collaboration.

The issue of men's involvement in women's rights is increasingly recognized as important, even at the highest level. Phumzile Mlambo-Ngcuka, United Nations under-secretary-general, issued a challenge to men on the occasion of International Women's Day 2014:

I know many of you desire a better world for women and girls and more than a few of you are actively working on bringing about positive changes. But there is much more to do. We need your action and your voices to be louder and to help us change some of the hardships women face. I invite you to join me and the women and men of the world who have led many long struggles for the gender equality. In Africa, we have a saying that I want to leave with you: 'If you go alone you go fast, but if we go together, we go far'. Let us go far together.[3]

This book has shown how and where men, collectively and individually, have been able to make that journey and to make a difference to women's lives – and thus to their own as well. It has looked at attitudes towards being male and female, and how these are shaped at an early age. It has examined the increased involvement of fathers in their children's lives – and how and why this benefits men, children and women as well. It has looked at some of the forces that militate against gender equality – violence against women being the most obvious, but also religious conservatism, the neoliberal agenda and the overt sexualization of women's bodies.

It has also shown that in so many areas of our lives – for example, health, education or employment – women's and men's organizing for gender equality are separate discourses that rarely come together. And that sometimes when they do, there is conflict.

Men and women need spaces to organize separately as well as together, but in the struggle to push back against the gender inequalities that lead to violence, sexualization, discrimination and violence, the many different voices need to be united. And there is still a long way to go.

We have seen how, in the past few decades, the lives of many women have changed beyond all recognition. They are continuing to change as women's rights and feminist movements struggle for equality.

Most men's lives have changed far less. It is as much the global economic realities of the day as any real desire for equality which are now forcing many men to re-evaluate their lives. They are struggling with some of the big questions about what masculinity means. And for this, they have little history to draw on. They have much to learn, not just from feminists and feminisms, but also from the LGBTI movement.

There is a small but growing movement of men for gender equality, but there also many men who cling to their power and privilege, and those who see feminists, and women's rights, as the enemy. This is why it is so important for all those who believe in gender equality and justice to work together rather than against each other or in separate silos.

Oswaldo Telleria Montoya of the MenEngage network is very clear about the benefits of equality for men: 'Not to buy into patriarchy means renouncing some historical privileges, but they are privileges which don't give you peace, don't give you happiness. What gives people happiness is being connected. If we continue with this gender asymmetry we are all in trouble.'[4]

Young British feminist Kat Banyard, author of *The Equality Illusion*, says: 'Feminism is an unfinished revolution. It remains one of the most important social justice movements of our age. Yes, there are stereotypes surrounding what feminism is and who feminists are. But that's because creating a world where women and men are equal isn't easy – it means challenging privilege and profit. Together we can bust those stereotypes and reclaim feminism for a new generation.'[5]

Together needs to include men as well. We have seen increasing numbers of men all over the world marching alongside women to protest against violence against women. This must continue to grow. We need men to be equally active in pushing for equality of opportunity at work, equal pay and economic justice. And they must be willing to challenge traditional models of masculinity in a variety of ways – for example, by participating fully in childcare and work in the home in order to give increasing numbers of women the opportunity to participate more fully in society. It is not only women but men themselves who will benefit.

Gender inequality deprives women of their rights and men of their humanity. A return to traditional versions of masculinity and femininity, however much religious conservatives and men's rights movements may want it, is not an option. Women will not go back into their boxes. It is men who now need to change; to give up some of their power and privilege in the interests of freeing themselves from the historically narrow model of what it means to be male.

I wrote in the first chapter about how my son's question about his place in the feminist story sparked the first ideas for this book. I don't want that question to remain hanging for the next generation of boys. It is time for feminism to actively include men, and for men to embrace feminism. The struggle for gender equality depends on it.

NOTES

1 Introduction

1 time.com/14543/calling-all-men-gender-equality-isnt-just-a-female-cause/.

2 *ICPD Beyond 2014 Global Report*, icpdbeyond2014.org/uploads/browser/files/icpd_global_review_report_12_feb_2014.pdf.

3 www.whiteribbon.com.

4 J. Prime and C. A. Moss-Racusin, *Engaging Men in Gender Initiatives: What Change Agents Need to Know*, Catalyst, 2009, www.catalyst.org/file/283/mdc-web.pdf.

5 www.heforshe.org/.

6 Interview with the author, 4 October 2013.

7 www.awid.org/.

8 Interview with the author.

9 www.menengage.org.

10 R. W. Connell, *Masculinities*, 2nd edn, Polity Press, Cambridge, 2005.

11 ukfeminista.org.uk/.

2 Beyond the binaries

1 www.theroot.com/views/why-i-am-male-feminist.

2 dlvr.it/44X6Mr.

3 www.netmums.com/home/feminism.

4 www.granta.com/New-Writing/Interview-Urvashi-Butalia.

5 *Feminist Theory from Margin to Center*, Pluto Press, 2000, and *Feminism Is for Everybody: Passionate Politics*, Pluto Press, 2000.

6 Ibid.

7 thefeministwire.com/2013/10/17973/; www.alternet.org/story/81260/on_prisons %2C_borders%2C_safety%2C_and_privilege%3 A_an_open_letter_to_white_feminists.

8 www.theguardian.com/commentisfree/2013/dec/09/black-feminist-movement-fails-women-black-minority.

9 thefeministwire.com/2014/01/i-am-a-girl/#.UtafoB9onhM.twitter.

10 Nancy Fraser, *Fortunes of Feminism: From State-Managed Capitalism to Neoliberal Crisis*, Verso, 2013.

11 www.theguardian.com/commentisfree/2013/oct/14/feminism-capitalist-handmaiden-neoliberal.

12 www.guardian.co.uk/education/2012/nov/23/why-is-feminism-a-dirty-word.

13 'Talk feminism: the F word and girls today', Guide Association, 2013.

14 Interview in Jakarta, February 2014.

15 Caitlin Moran, *How to Be a Woman*, HarperCollins, 2012.

16 Committee for Economic Development of Australia (CEDA), *Women in Leadership: Understanding the gender gap*, 2013.

17 whoneedsfeminism.tumblr.com/.

18 ukfeminista.org.uk/.

19 promundo.org.br/en/.

20 newint.org/features/2011/

07/01/boys-brazils-favelas-violence-against-women/.

21 Interview with the author, February 2014.

22 www.feminist.com/askamy/feminism/0309_femo6.html.

23 Allan G. Johnson, *The Gender Knot: Unravelling our patriarchal legacy*, Temple University Press, 2005.

24 www.contestations.net/issues/issue-3/women%E2%80%99s-empowerment-what-do-men-have-to-do-with-it/.

25 L. Penny, 'Of course all men don't hate women. But all men must know they benefit from sexism', www.newstatesman.com/2013/08/laurie-penny/men-sexism.

26 Interview, June 2013. Melanie blogs on www.queery.oia.co.za; and www.thoughtleader.co.za/melanie judge.

27 onlinelibrary.wiley.com/doi/10.1111/1759-5436.12074/abstract.

28 Michael Kimmel, 'Who's afraid of men doing feminism?', in Tom Digby (ed.), *Men Doing Feminism*, Routledge, 1998.

29 www.bbc.co.uk/news/world-africa-25775002.

30 www.europarl.europa.eu/news/en/news-room/content/2013 0508STO08096/html/Day- against-homophobia-new-survey-reveals-scale-of-discrimination-in-Europe; and newint.org/blog/2013 /05/17/homophobia-europe/#sthash.aY92 NYOd.dpuf.

31 edition.cnn.com/2013/05/23/opinion/opinion-poirier-same-sex-marriage-suicide/index.html.

32 Ibid.

33 'Forbidden discourse: the silencing of feminist criticism of "gender": an open statement from 37 radical feminists from five countries',

12 August 2013, www.pandagon.net/wp-content/uploads/2013/08/GENDER-Statement.pdf?f9e4e1.

34 feministsfightingtransphobia.wordpress.com/2013/09/16/a-statement-of-trans-inclusive-feminism/.

35 msmagazine.com/blog/2012/04/18/trans-feminism-theres-no-conundrum-about-it/.

36 www.guardian.co.uk/education/2012/nov/23/why-is-feminism-a-dirty-word.

37 www.theguardian.com/uk-news/2013/sep/03/caroline-criado-perez-rape-threats-continue.

38 www.ew.com/ew/article/0,,20679716,00.html.

39 feminismbelongs.tumblr.com/.

40 Susan Faludi, *Stiffed: The Betrayal of the Modern Man*, Chatto and Windus, 1999.

41 Hanna Roisin, *The End of Men and the Rise of Women*, Penguin/Viking, 2012.

42 Faludi, *Stiffed*.

43 Warren Farrell, *The Myth of Male Power*, Simon and Schuster, 1993.

44 www.avoiceformen.com/.

45 www.avoiceformen.com/a-voice-for-men/understanding-the-mens-rights-movement/.

46 Faludi, *Stiffed*.

47 Ibid.

48 Interview with the author.

49 J. A. Prime and C. A. Moss-Racusin, *Engaging Men in Gender Initiatives: What Change Agents Need to Know*, Catalyst, 2009, www.catalyst.org/file/283/mdc-web.pdf.

50 blogs.independent.co.uk/2012/07/23/how-should-we-talk-to-men-about-sexism/.

51 www.theguardian.com/commentisfree/2013/aug/06/male-feminism-hugo-schwyzer.

52 brightonmanplan.wordpress.
com/2012/03/19/a-new-gender-
agenda-by-glen-poole-part-3/.

53 Rebecca Kamm, 'Kiwi men talk
about feminism', *New Zealand Herald*,
21 June 2013, www.nzherald.co.nz/
lifestyle/news/article.cfm?c_id=6&
objectid=10892026.

54 www.menengage.org/.

55 N. van der Gaag et al.,
'Because I am a girl: so what about
boys? State of the world's girls', Plan
International, 2011.

56 R. W. Connell, 'Change among
the gatekeepers: men, masculinities,
and gender equality in the global
arena', *Signs*, 30, 2005, pp. 1801–25.

57 newint.org/fea-
tures/2011/07/01/boys-brazils-favelas-
violence-against-women/.

58 socialmovements.bridge.ids.
ac.uk/sites/socialmovements.bridge.
ids.ac.uk/files/case-studies/Marc%
20Peters%20-%20Reflecting%20
on%20the%20Oppressor%20in%
20the%20Mirror.pdf.

59 www.whiteribbon.com.

60 Michael Kaufman, 'Men,
feminism, and men's contradictory
experiences of power', in Joseph A.
Kuypers (ed.), *Men and Power*, Fernwood Books, Halifax, 1999, pp. 59–83.
A revised version of an article that
first appeared in Harry Brod and
Michael Kaufman (eds), *Theorizing
Masculinities*, Sage Publications,
1994, www.michaelkaufman.com/
wp-content/uploads/2009/01/men_
feminism.pdf.

3 Shifting cultural and social attitudes

1 Presentation at MenCare
conference, Cape Town, South Africa,
June 2013.

2 Cordelia Fine, *Delusions of
Gender: The Real Science behind Sex
Differences*, Icon Books, London, 2010.

3 Ibid.

4 Christophe Z. Guilmoto
'Sex imbalances at birth: current
trends, consequences and policy
implications', UNFPA Asia and Pacific
Regional Office, 2012; A. Sen, 'Missing
women', *British Medical Journal*, 304,
March 1992, ucatlas.ucsc.edu/gender/
Sen100M.html.

5 newint.org/features/2013/10/
01/girls-not-allowed-keynote/#sthash.
qknJKJAZ.dpuf.

6 J. Evans, *Both Halves of the
Sky: Gender Socialization in the Early
Years*, Consultative Group on Early
Childhood Care and Development,
1997, www.ecdgroup.com/download/
cc120abi.pdf.

7 *Ethiopia: Creating Partnerships
to Prevent Early Marriage in the
Amhara Region*, Pathfinder International, July 2006.

8 *Behind the Screen*, Plan Asia,
2008.

9 Ibid.

10 United Nations Department of
Public Information, DPI/1772/HR.

11 *The Girl Child: Beijing at 10:
putting policy into practice*, INSTRAW,
2004.

12 www.becauseiamagirl.org.

13 Irada Gautam, 'The difficulties
girls face in families, in Ramghat and
Ghusra villages of Surkhet District,
mid-western Nepal', Save the Children
(UK) Office for South and Central
Asia Region Kathmandu, May 1999.
http://www.savethechildren.org.uk/
scuk_cache/scuk/cache/cmsattach/
605_nepalgenderreport.pdf

14 Evans, *Both Halves of the Sky*.

15 Women's Commission for Refugee Women and Children, *Masculin-*

ities: *Male Roles and Male Involvement in the Promotion of Gender Equality: Resource Packet*, 2005.

16 Evans, *Both Halves of the Sky*.

17 Kirrily Pells, 'Young Lives findings on gender', unpublished background paper written for Plan International, 2011; Young Lives, 'Because I Am a Girl', Oxford, 2011, younglives.org.uk.

18 Pells, 'Young Lives findings on gender'.

19 Evans, *Both Halves of the Sky*.

20 'Tough Guise', abridged version of 'Violence, media and the crisis in masculinity', Media Education Foundation, 1999.

21 In 2007, the toy industry in the USA was valued at $3.2 billion: Department of Commerce, *Industry Report Dolls, Toys, Games, and Children's Vehicles*, NAICS Code 33993, 21 October 2008, citing 2004, 2005 and 2006 Annual Survey of Manufactures, US Census Bureau.

22 www.pinkstinks.co.uk/.

23 Adapted from Jon Henley, 'The power of pink', Guardian, 12 December 2009, www.guardian.co.uk/theguardian/2009/dec/12/pinkstinks-the-power-of-pink.

24 www.pinkstinks.co.uk/voices.php.

25 www.pinkstinks.org.uk/our-campaigns.html.

26 www.lettoysbetoys.org.uk/.

27 www.lettoysbetoys.org.uk/the-let-toys-be-toys-2013-silliness-awards/#more-1901.

28 Nikki van der Gaag et al., 'Because I am a girl: so what about boys? State of the world's girls', Plan International, 2011.

29 Ministry of Education, 'National Policy on Integrated Growth and Development for Early Child

hood', 1st edn, p. 24, in El Salvador's Country Strategic Plan 2012–2016, 2010.

30 www.guardian.co.uk/theguardian/2009/dec/12/pinkstinks-the-power-of-pink.

31 'Tough Guise'.

32 G. Barker, J. M. Contreras, B. Heilman, A. K. Singh, R. K. Verma and M. Nascimento, *Evolving Men: Initial Results from the International Men and Gender Equality Survey (IMAGES)*, International Center for Research on Women (ICRW), Washington, DC, and Instituto Promundo, Rio de Janeiro, January 2011.

33 Niobe Way, *Deep Secrets: Boys' friendships and the crisis of connection*, Harvard University Press, 2011, pp. 2, 3 and 21.

34 Joseph H. Pleck, Freya L. Sonenstein, Leighton C. Ku, 'Masculinity ideology: its impact on adolescent males' heterosexual relationships', *Journal of Social Issues*, 49(3), Fall 1993, pp. 11–29.

35 Lise Eliot, *Pink Brain, Blue Brain: How Small Differences Grow into Troublesome Gaps – and What We Can Do about It*, Mariner Books, New York, 2010.

36 www.men-care.org.

37 www.stonewall.org.uk/what_we_do/at_school/education_for_all/3839.asp.

38 Barker et al., *Evolving Men*.

39 www.theguardian.com/world/2013/dec/20/uganda-mps-laws-homosexuality.

40 www.pewsocialtrends.org/2013/06/13/a-survey-of-lgbt-americans/.

41 'Tough Guise'.

42 www.ew.com/ew/article/0,,20679716,00.html.

43 American Psychological

Association, *Report of the APA Task Force on the Sexualization of Girls*, Washington, DC, 2007, www.apa.org/pi/wpo/sexualization.html.

44 www.sparksummit.com/.

45 www.huffingtonpost.co.uk/2013/07/02/barbie-as-a-normal-woman_n_3534934.html.

46 www.platform51.org/downloads/resources/briefings/obesity.pdf.

47 Cited in Plan, 'Because I am a girl', 2007.

48 Jenny Langley, *Boys Get Anorexia Too: Coping with Male Eating Disorders in the Family*, Sage Publications, 2006.

49 A. Bridges, R. Wosnitzer, E. Scharrer, C. Sun and R. Liberman (forthcoming), 'Aggression and sexual behavior in best-selling pornography: a content analysis update', Violence Against Women. See also www.internetsafety101.org/Pornography statistics.htm.

50 R. J. Wosnitzer and A. J. Bridges, 'Aggression and sexual behavior in best-selling pornography: a content analysis update', Paper presented at the 57th Annual Meeting of the International Communication Association, San Francisco, CA, 2007.

51 www.theguardian.com/world/2003/nov/08/gender.weekend7.

52 Michael Flood, 'Harms of pornography exposure among children and young people', *Child Abuse Review*, 18(6), November/December 2009.

53 Maurice Chittenden and Matthew Holehouse, 'Boys who see porn more likely to harass girls', *Sunday Times*, 24 January 2010.

54 Robert Stoller, *Porn: Myths for the Twentieth Century*, Yale University Press, 1991.

55 www.theguardian.com/world/2003/nov/08/gender.week end7.

56 Ana J. Bridges, 'Pornography's effects on interpersonal relationships', n.d., www.socialcostsofpornography.com/Bridges_Pornographys_Effect_on_Interpersonal_Relationships.pdf.

57 Center for Disease & Control, *Internet Solutions for Kids*, November 2010.

58 E. Häggström-Nordin, U. Hanson and T. Tydén, 'Associations between pornography consumption and sexual practices among adolescents in Sweden', *International Journal of STD and AIDS*, 16, 2005, pp. 102–7.

59 Jessica Valenti, *Full Frontal Feminism: A Young woman's guide to why feminism matters*, Seal Press, 2007.

60 Adapted from Kira Cochrane, 'The men who believe porn is wrong', Guardian, 28 October 2010, www.theguardian.com/culture/2010/oct/25/men-believe-porn-is-wrong.

61 www.theguardian.com/lifeandstyle/2010/apr/15/nawal-el-saadawi-egyptian-feminist.

62 Cassandra Balchin, *Religious Fundamentalisms on the Rise: A case for action*, AWID, 2008, www.awid.org/Media/Files/RFs-on-the-Rise-A-case-for-action.

63 www.addictinginfo.org/2012/04/09/pat-robertson-women-are-subservient-to-men-in-marriage-video/.

64 Senhorina Wendoh and Tina Wallace, 'Living gender in African organisations and communities: stories from the Gambia, Rwanda, Uganda and Zambia', Transform Africa, 2006.

65 Balchin, *Religious Fundamentalisms on the Rise*.

66 www.equalityiniraq.com/

articles/158--is-international-womens-day-still-worth-celebrating-.

67 www.sistersinislam.org.my/.

68 www.theguardian.com/commentisfree/2007/jan/29/islamic feminismonthemove.

69 www.theguardian.com/commentisfree/2007/jan/29/islamic feminismonthemove.

70 news.bbc.co.uk/1/hi/world/europe/4384512.stm.

71 www.bbc.co.uk/news/world-middle-east-23246295.

72 Claire Read, BBC Arabic Service, Cairo, www.bbc.co.uk/news/world-middle-east-23246295.

73 International Society for Human Rights. 'Interview with Amir Rashidi: Iran ignores the economic contribution of women', n.d., www.ishr.org/Interview-with-Amir-Rashidi.1386.o.html.

74 www.men-care.org/Media/Films-From-MenCare-Partners.aspx.

75 www.thejakartapost.com/news/2013/12/15/healthy-happy-wives-begin-with-caring-men.html.

76 Ana Maria Munoz Boudet, Patti Petesch and Carolyn Turk with Angelica Thumala, 'On norms and agency conversations about gender equality with women and men in 20 countries', World Bank, 2012.

77 Barker et al., *Evolving Men*.

78 Munoz Boudet et al., 'On norms and agency …'.

79 Ibid.

80 Michael Kaufman, in Sandy Ruxton (ed.), *Gender Equality and Men: Learning from Practice*, Oxfam GB, 2004.

81 great-men-value-women.tumblr.com/about.

82 www.bbc.co.uk/programmes/bo3b2v6p.

83 Leisa Sánchez, 'Young men break with machista stereotypes in Ecuador', www.ipsnews.net/2013/05/youngsters-break-with-machista-stereotypes-in-ecuador.

4 No zero-sum game

1 www.bbc.co.uk/programmes/bo3nrm2o.

2 V. Filippi, C. Ronsmans, O. Campbell et al., 'Maternal health in poor countries: the broader context and a call for action', *The Lancet*, 368, 2006, pp. 1535–41.

3 www.unfpa.org/gender/empowerment2.htm.

4 UNESCO Institute for Statistics, 'Persistence to last grade of primary, female (as % of cohort)', World Development Indicators, data.worldbank.org/indicator/SE.PRM.PRSL.FE.ZS.

5 Jessica Shepherd, 'Girls think they are cleverer than boys from age four, study finds', *Guardian*, 1 September 2010.

6 Gary Barker, Manuel Contreras, Brian Heilman, Ajay Singh, Ravi Verma and Marcos Nascimento, 'Evolving men: initial results from the international men and gender equality survey', International Center for Research on Women and Instituto Promundo, 2011.

7 www.who.int/features/qa/12/en.

8 www.un.org/millenniumgoals/maternal.shtml.

9 hdr.undp.org/en/statistics/gii/.

10 A. Hawkes and K. Buse, 'Gender and global health: evidence, policy, and inconvenient truths', *The Lancet*, 381, 2013, pp. 1783–87.

11 Nikki van der Gaag et al., 'Because I am girl 2013: in double jeopardy: girls in disasters', *State of the World's Girls*, Plan International, 2013.

12 www.pakistantoday.com.
pk/2011/11/26/comment/editors-mail/
lack-of-literacy-in-pakistan/.

13 UNDP, *Human Development Report*, 2011.

14 www.pakistantoday.com.
pk/2011/11/26/comment/editors-mail/
lack-of-literacy-in-pakistan/.

15 UNESCO, 'Gender achievements and prospects in education', Gap report, Part One, UNICEF, 2005.

16 Featured in Nikki van der Gaag et al., 'Because I am a girl – the state of the world's girls 2011: so what about boys?', Plan International, 2011.

17 Trefor Lloyd, 'Young men's attitude to gender and work', Joseph Rowntree, May 1999.

18 Naomi Hossain, 'School exclusion as social exclusion: the practices and effects of a conditional cash transfer programme for the poor in Bangladesh', Chronic Poverty Research Centre Working Paper 148, June 2009.

19 World Bank, *Vietnam High Quality Education for All by 2020*, Washington, DC: World Bank, 2011.

20 Alexandra Smith, 'Feminized curriculum "has thrown boy out with bathwater"', *Guardian*, 13 June 2006; 'Failing boys' series: part 6 'We can't tolerate failing boys', *Globe and Mail*, 21 October 2010.

21 Kate Hammer, 'Role models: one of five reasons why boys are failing', National News, *Globe and Mail*, 15 October 2010.

22 Caine Rolleston, Zoe James, Laure Pasquier-Doumer and Tran Ngo Thi Minh Tam 'Making progress: report of the Young Lives school survey in Vietnam' (2013) Working Paper 100, Young Lives, Oxford.

23 UNESCO, 'Gender achievements and prospects in education'.

24 Van der Gaag et al., 'Because I am a girl'.

25 Caine Rolleston, Zoe James, Laure Pasquier-Doumer and Tran Ngo Thi Minh Tam, 'Making progress: report of the Young Lives School Survey in Vietnam', Working Paper 100, Young Lives, 2013, www.younglives.org.uk/publications/WP/making-progress-report-of-the-young-lives-school-survey-in-vietnam.

26 World Bank, *Vietnam High Quality Education for All by 2020*.

27 UNESCO. 'EFA Global Monitoring Report: Reaching the marginalised', Oxford University Press, 2010.

28 General Teaching Council for England, *Annual Digest of Statistics 2009–10*.

29 Instituto Promundo, 'Approximate numbers from internal conversations with the Rio de Janeiro government staff members', Rio de Janeiro, 2010.

30 Gary Barker, in collaboration with Margaret Greene and Nascimento Marcos, 'Men Who Care: A multi-country qualitative study of men in non-traditional caregiving roles', Men and Gender Equality Policy Project (MGEPP), led by Instituto Promundo and the International Center for Research on Women (ICRW), 2012.

31 Victoria J. Rideout, Ulla G. Foehr and Donald F. Roberts, 'Generation M2: media in the lives of 8- to 18-year-olds', Henry J. Kaiser Family Foundation, Menlo Park, CA, 2010.

32 'Failing boys series: Part 6'.

33 Gary Barker, *Dying to Be Men: Youth, Masculinity and Social Exclusion*, Routledge, 2005.

34 Ibid.

35 UNESCO, 'Gender achievements and prospects in education'.

36 University of the West Indies.

'The story of four schools: findings of the Change from Within project initiated at the University of the West Indies', Mona: University Printers, 1999; Hyacinth Evans, 'Gender and achievement in secondary education in Jamaica', in *Jamaica Survey of Living Conditions*, 2001; L. Blank, 'Youth at risk in Jamaica', based on Jamaican research and statistics, OECD, Programme for the Improvement of Student Assessment (PISA) id21 Research Highlight, 12 September 2003.

37 Peta-Anne Barker, 'Public affairs, tackling school violence', Commentary, *Jamaica Gleaner News*, 29 August 2010.

38 Gillian Gaynair, 'Parivartan works with boys and young men to reduce violence against women', News and Commentary, ICRW Media, 26 May 2010.

39 www.huffingtonpost.com/ dr-madhumita-das/using-cricket-to-talk-abo_b_1734428.html.

40 Ibid.

41 Plan International, 'Because I am a girl', 2010 cohort.

42 www.icrw.org/where-we-work/ gender-equity-movement-schools-gems.

43 Margaret Greene and Andrew Levack, 'Synchronizing gender strategies: a cooperative model for improving reproductive health and transforming gender relations', for the Interagency Gender Working Group (IGWG), 2010.

44 Pew Research Center: Spring 2010 survey.

45 Hammer, 'Role models'.

46 www.pewglobal.org/2013/01/ 04/indians-support-gender-equality-but-still-give-men-edge-in-workplace-higher-education/.

47 hdr.undp.org/en/.

48 hdr.undp.org/en/statistics/ gii/.

49 Hawkes and Buse, 'Gender and global health'.

50 R. Lozano, M. Naghavi, K. Foreman et al., 'Global and regional mortality from 235 causes of death for 20 age groups in 1990 and 2010: a systematic analysis of the Global Burden of Disease Study 2010', *The Lancet*, 380, 2012, pp. 2095–128, quoted in Hawkes and Buse, 'Gender and global health'.

51 C. J. L. Murray, M. Ezzatti, A. Flaxman et al., 'GBD 2010: design, definitions, and metrics', *The Lancet*, 380, 2012, pp. 2063–6, quoted in Hawkes and Buse, 'Gender and global health'.

52 W. H. Courtenay, 'Better to die than cry? A longitudinal and constructionist study of masculinity and the health risk behavior of young American men', Doctoral dissertation, University of California at Berkeley, Dissertation Abstracts International, 1998.

53 M. Foreman (ed.), *AIDS and Men: Taking Risks or Taking Responsibility*, Zed Books, London, 1999.

54 Barker, *Dying to Be Men*.

55 Ibid.

56 *Mortality Stats by Cause, England and Wales*, www.ons.go.uk, 2011.

57 www.theguardian.com/society/ 2014/feb/18/male-suicides-three-times-women-samaritans-bristol.

58 UNDP, *Human Development Report 2013*.

59 news.bbc.co.uk/2/hi/uk_news/ 7219232.stm.

60 *In Their Own Right: Addressing the sexual and reproductive health needs of men worldwide*, Alan Guttmacher Institute, 2002.

61 Reported in *Young Men's Sexual*

and Reproductive Health: Toward a National Strategy, www.urban.org/uploadedpdf/410027.pdf.

62 UNICEF, State of the World's Children, 2011.

63 UNAIDS, UNAIDS World AIDS Day Report 2011. How to Get to Zero: Faster. Smarter. Better, Stylus Publications LLC, VA, 2011.

64 Orly Stern, Dean Peacock and Helen Alexander, Working with Men and Boys: Emerging strategies from across Africa to address gender-based violence and HIV/AIDS, Sonke Gender Justice Network and the MenEngage Network, 2009.

65 Emily Esplen, 'Engaging men in gender equality: positive strategies and approaches overview and annotated bibliography', Bibliography no. 15, Bridge. 2006.

66 Jonny Steinberg, Sizwe's Test: A Young Man's Journey through Africa's AIDS Epidemic, Simon and Schuster, 2008.

67 Stern et al., Working with Men and Boys.

68 L. Johnson, 'Access to antiretroviral treatment in South Africa, 2004–2011', South Afr. J. HIV Med, 13(1), 2012.

69 P. Braitstein, A. Boulle, D. Nash et al., 'Gender and the use of antiretroviral treatment in resource-constrained settings: findings from a multicenter collaboration', J. Women's Health (Larchmt), 17(1), 2008, pp. 47–55.

70 Njoki Wainaina, 'The role of African men in the fight against HIV/AIDS', Paper presented at the Expert Group Meeting on 'The role of men and boys in achieving gender equality', Brasilia, October 2003.

71 Hawkes and Buse, 'Gender and global health'.

72 www.ipsnews.net/2012/11/how-african-men-are-changing-traditional-beliefs/.

73 Greene and Levack, 'Synchronizing gender strategies'.

74 Alan Greig, Dean Peacock, Rachel Jewkes and Sisonke Mismang, 'Gender and AIDS: Time to act', AIDS 2008, 22(2): 37, citing T. Wallace, Evaluating Stepping Stones: A Review of Existing Evaluations and Ideas for Future M&E Work, ActionAid International, London, 2006.

75 Sidney Ruth Schuler, 'Gender and community participation in reproductive health projects: contrasting models from Peru and Ghana', Reproductive Health Matters, 7(14), 1999, pp. 144–57.

76 Delicia Ferrando, Nery Serrano and Carlos Pure, 'Perú: salud reproductiva en comunidades. Educando y empoderando a mujeres de escasos recursos: evaluación de impacto de medio término del proyecto ReproSalud', Monitoring, Evaluation, and Design Support Project, Peru, 2002.

77 www.promundo.org.br/en/sem-categoria/entre-nos-campanha/.

78 Greene and Levack, 'Synchronizing gender strategies'.

5 Giving up power?

1 www.theatlantic.com/magazine/archive/2010/07/the-end-of-men/308135/.

2 H. Boushey, 'The new breadwinners', in H. Boushey and A. O'Leary (eds), The Shriver Report. A woman's nation changes everything, Center for American Progress, Washington, DC, 2009, pp. 30–67.

3 N. Kabeer, The Power to Choose: Bangladeshi Women and Labour

Market Decisions in London and Dhaka, Verso, London, 2000.

4 Ruth Pearson, 'Gender, globalisation and the reproduction of labour: bringing the state back in', in Shirin M. Rai and Georgina Waylen (eds), *New Frontiers in Feminist Political Economy*, Routledge, 2013.

5 ideas.time.com/2013/03/07/confidence-woman/#ixzz2aWXwOcD9.

6 www.stephaniecoontz.com/articles/article97.htm.

7 Global Partnership for Financial Inclusion and International Finance Corporation, 'Strengthening access to finance for women-owned SMEs in developing countries', International Finance Corporation, Washington, DC, October 2011, www1.ifc.org/wps/wcm/connect/a4774a004a3f66539f0f9f8969adcc27/G20_Women_Report.pdf?MOD=AJPERES.

8 wiego.org/informal-economy/statistical-picture.

9 UN Women and ILO, 'Policy brief. Decent work and women's economic empowerment: good policy and practice', 2012, www.unwomen.org/wp-content/uploads/2012/08/decent-work-and-women-economic-empowement_policybrief.pdf.

10 World Bank, 'Women are less likely than men to participate in the labour market in most countries', 2012, data.worldbank.org/news/women-less-likely-than-men-to-participate-in-labor-market.

11 Ibid.

12 www.forbes.com/sites/margiewarrell/2013/05/03/whats-keeping-so-many-smart-women-from-climbing-the-ladder/.

13 www.catalyst.org/knowledge/women-ceos-fortune-1000.

14 European Commission – Directorate-General for Justice, 'Women and men in leadership positions in the European Union 2013: a review of the situation and recent progress', 2013.

15 S. Nkomo and H. Ngambi, 'African women in leadership: current knowledge and a framework for future studies', *International Journal of African Renaissance Studies*, 4(1), 2009, pp. 49–68. Quoted in T. Wallace and H. Banos-Smith, 'The context for IIEP research on women in senior management', International Institute for Educational Planning (IIEP), UNESCO, Paris, 2011, www.iiep.unesco.org/research/challenges-and-emerging-trends/post-2015/gender-equality.html.

16 'Women in senior management: setting the stage for growth', Grant Thornton International Business Report, 2013.

17 Ibid.

18 www.ipu.org/wmn-e/world.htm.

19 www.unwomen.org/en/news/stories/2014/3/progress-for-women-in-politics-but-glass-ceiling-remains-firm.

20 www.youtube.com/watch?v=IA6y44JgThE.

21 www.trust.org/slideshow/?id=2abcocd9-bd82-4d2d-9ddc-3e85e82e5803.

22 Claudia Goldin and Lawrence F. Katz, 'Gender differences in careers, education, and games transitions: career and family life cycles of the educational elite', *American Economic Review: Papers & Proceedings*, 98(2), 2008, pp. xx–xx, www.aeaweb.org/articles.php?doi=10.1257/aer.98.2.xx.

23 World Bank, 'Ready for work: increasing economic opportunity for adolescent girls and young women', n.d.

24 UN Women and ILO, 'Policy brief. Decent work and women's economic empowerment'.

25 www.americanprogress.org/issues/labor/news/2012/04/16/11391/the-top-10-facts-about-the-wage-gap/.

26 www.weforum.org/news/slow-progress-closing-global-economic-gender-gap-new-major-study-finds.

27 www.fawcettsociety.org.uk/new-report-warns-of-female-unfriendly-labour-market-as-womens-unemployment-continues-to-rise/#sthash.oas4J7rE.dpuf.

28 ILO, 'Report of the Director General. A new era of social justice', International Labour Conference, 100th Session, ILO, Geneva, 2011.

29 See n. 27.

30 World Bank, 'Ready for work'.

31 Plan, 'Paying the price, the economic cost of failing to educate girls', Plan, Woking, 2008, referring to World Bank research and economic data and UNESCO education statistics.

32 www.newstatesman.com/economics/2014/02/gender-inequality-costing-global-economy-trillions-dollars-year.

33 Hanna Roisin, *The End of Men – and the Rise of Women*, Penguin/Viking, 2012, www.theatlantic.com/magazine/archive/2010/07/the-end-of-men/308135/.

34 See, for example, A. Oakley, *Housewife*, Allen Lane, London, 1974, republished by Pelican.

35 Gary Barker, *Dying to Be Men: Youth masculinities and social exclusion*, Routledge, London, 2005.

36 Ibid.

37 Source for Momodou: Senorina Wendoh and Tina Wallace, 'Living gender in African organisations and communities: stories from the Gam-

bia, Rwanda, Uganda and Zambia', Transform Africa report, May 2006, p. 62; Source for remaining quotes: Barker, *Dying to Be Men*.

38 Roisin, *The End of Men*.

39 Wendoh and Wallace, 'Living gender in African organisations and communities', p. 62.

40 ILO, 'Facts about women and work'.

41 Interviews with the author, quoted in Nikki van der Gaag et al., 'Because I am a girl: so what about boys? The state of the world's girls 2011', Plan International.

42 Information from Oxfam, 'Trading away our rights: women working in global supply chains', Oxfam International, Oxford, 2004, in Kate Grosser and Nikki van der Gaag, 'Can girls save the world', in Tina Wallace, Fenella Porter and Mark Ralph-Bowman, 'Aid, NGOs and the realities of women's lives: a perfect storm', Practical Action, 2013.

43 www.waronwant.org/attachments/Up%20Front%20%20Sweatshops%20and%20the%20Olympics.pdf.

44 www.ids.ac.uk/project/life-in-a-time-of-food-price-volatility.

45 Naomi Hossain, 'Poor man's patriarchy', draft paper for the Undressing Patriarchy symposium, Brighton, 9–12 September 2013, IDS, Sussex.

46 'Extreme poverty and human rights', GA Res. 17/13, UN GAOR, 68th Sess., U.N. Doc. A/68/293, 2013.

47 ideas.time.com/2013/03/07/why-i-want-women-to-lean-in/#ixzz2a A4UKkVU.

48 http://www.mckinsey.com/client_service/organization/latest_thinking/unlocking_the_full_potential.

49 www.npr.org/2013/04/22/17

7511506/want-more-gender-equality-at-work-go-to-an-emerging-market.

50 Felicity Butler and Catherine Hoskyns, newint.org/blog/2013/08/12/paid-domestic-work-nicaragua/#sthash.FugWB8ga.dpuf.

51 Sandberg, *Lean In*.

52 'Women Matter 2013: Gender diversity in top management: moving corporate cultures, moving boundaries', www.mckinsey.com/insights/organization/moving_mind-sets_on_gender_diversity_mckinsey_ global_survey_results?goback=.gde_2216278_member_583772996 9224060928.

53 CEDA, 'Women in leadership: understanding the gender gap', June 2013.

54 /www.nytimes.com/2013/09/18/world/asia/for-china-a-new-kind-of-feminism.html?ref=women&_r=2&.

55 Naila Kabeer, 'Women's economic empowerment and inclusive growth: labour markets and enterprise development', SIG WORKING PAPER 2012/1, IDRC and DfID.

56 Wallace and Banos-Smith, 'The context for IIEP research on women in senior management'.

57 Ibid.

58 L. Chisholm, 'Gender and leadership in South Africa educational administration', *Gender and Education*, 13(4), 2001, pp. 387–99.

59 tech.fortune.cnn.com/2013/04/30/the-biggest-deterrent-for-women-in-tech/.

60 CEDA, 'Women in leadership'.

61 Pew Research Center, Spring 2013 survey.

62 www.theguardian.com/commentisfree/2014/jan/21/lord-rennard-why-sexual-harassment-matters.

63 Kabeer, 'Women's economic empowerment and inclusive growth'.

64 www.pewglobal.org/2013/01/04/indians-support-gender-equality-but-still-give-men-edge-in-workplace-higher-education/.

65 www.pewglobal.org/files/2010/07/Pew-Global-Attitudes-2010-Gender-Report-July-1-12-01AM-EDT-NOT-EMBARGOED.pdf.

66 R. Habib, I. Nuwayhid and J. Yeretzian, 'Paid work and domestic labour in disadvantaged communities on the outskirts of Beirut, Lebanon', *Sex Roles; a Journal of Research*, 55(5/6), September 2006, pp. 321–9. Quoted in T. Wallace, 'Women's work in Lebanon: making the invisible visible', CRTD, Beirut, Lebanon, 2013.

67 Nancy Fraser, *Fortunes of Feminism: From State-managed Capitalism to Neoliberal Crisis*, Verso, 2013.

68 P. Mainardi, 'The politics of housework', in R. Morgan (ed.), *Sisterhood Is Powerful*, Vintage Books, 1970. See more at: newint.org/features/1988/03/05/wages/#sthash.wLSYs4Pe.dpuf, and for a discussion of the controversy see newint.org/features/1988/03/05/wages/.

69 www.men-care.org/10-MenCare-Themes/2002E-Share-the-Care-Work.aspx.

70 Henny Slegh, Gary Barker, Augustin Kimonyo, Prudence Ndolimana and Matt Bannerman, '"I can do women's work": reflections on engaging men as allies in women's economic empowerment in Rwanda', *Gender & Development*, 21(1), 2013, pp. 15–30; doi: 10.1080/13552074.2013.767495.

71 Ibid.

72 www.nytimes.com/2013/09/18/world/asia/for-china-a-new-kind-of-feminism.html?ref=women&_r=2&.

73 Kabeer, 'Women's economic empowerment and inclusive growth'.

74 www.stephaniecoontz.com/articles/article97.htm.

75 Pearson, 'Gender, globalisation and the reproduction of labour'.

76 http://www.nytimes.com/2013/02/17/opinion/sunday/why-gender-equality-stalled.html?pagewanted=all&_r=1&

77 www.styleite.com/news/read-beyonces-essay-on-gender-equality/.

6 The fatherhood revolution?

1 www.men-care.org/Media/MenCare-Films.aspx.

2 www.whitehouse.gov/administration/eop/ofbnp/policy/fatherhood.

3 G. Barker, J. M. Contreras, B. Heilman, A. K. Singh, R. K. Verma and M. Nascimento, *Evolving Men: Initial Results from the International Men and Gender Equality Survey (IMAGES)*, International Center for Research on Women (ICRW), Washington, DC, and Instituto Promundo, Rio de Janeiro, 2011.

4 www.xyonline.net/content/hand-rocks-cradle.

5 www.fira.ca/article.php?id=44.

6 www.whitehouse.gov/administration/eop/ofbnp/policy/fatherhood.

7 www.men-care.org.

8 A. Gavanas, 'The fatherhood responsibility movement: the centrality of marriage, work and male sexuality in reconstructions of masculinity and fatherhood', in *Making Men into Fathers*, Cambridge University Press, 2002.

9 www.pewsocialtrends.org/2013/03/14/modern-parenthood-roles-of-moms-and-dads-converge-as-they-balance-work-and-family/.

10 www.fira.ca/article.php?id=44.

11 Sandy Ruxton and Nikki van der Gaag, *The Involvement of Men in Gender Equality Initiatives in the European Union*, European Institute for Gender Equality (EIGE), 2012.

12 Barker et al., *Evolving Men*.

13 www.ilo.org/wcmsp5/groups/public/---ed_protect/---protrav/--travail/documents/presentation/wcms_146268.pdf.

14 www.theatlantic.com/magazine/archive/2014/01/the-daddy-track/355746/.

15 www.btplc.com/news/articles/showarticle.cfm?articleid={c66e1862-1b1c-4bbb-8a3d-20fad960e7b6}.

16 World Bank, *World Development Report 2012: Gender Equality and Development*, World Bank, 2012.

17 www.nytimes.com/2013/07/10/world/europe/When-Dad-Becomes-the-Lead-Parent.html?_r=4&goback=.gde_978927_member_257894877&.

18 Gary Barker and Fabio Verani, 'Men's participation as fathers in the Latin American and Caribbean region: a critical literature review with policy considerations', Promundo and Save the Children, 2008.

19 E. A. Johansson, 'The effect of own and spousal parental leave on earnings', Working Paper Series 4, IFAU – Institute for Evaluation of Labour Market and Education Policy, 2010.

20 iloblog.org/2013/07/08/work-and-family-a-crucial-balance/.

21 A. M. Boudet, P. Petesch and C. Turk, with A. Thumala, 'On norms and agency: conversations about gender equality with women and men in 20 countries', World Bank Group, 2012.

22 Ibid.

23 www.pewsocialtrends.org/2013/12/11/on-pay-gap-millennial-women-near-parity-for-now/.

24 www.pewglobal.org/files/
2010/07/Pew-Global-Attitudes-2010-
Gender-Report-July-1-12-01AM-EDT-
NOT-EMBARGOED.pdf.

25 Brad Harrington, Fred van
Deusen and Beth Humberd, *The
New Dad: Caring, Committed and
Conflicted*, Boston College, 2011.

26 www.fira.ca/article.php?id=44.

27 www.pewsocialtrends.
org/2013/03/14/modern-parenthood-
roles-of-moms-and-dads-converge-as-
they-balance-work-and-family/.

28 www.pewresearch.org/fact-
tank/2013/07/10/for-young-adults-
the-ideal-marriage-meets-reality/.

29 Michael Flood, Judith Kegan
Gardiner, Bob Pease and Keith Pringle
(eds), *International Encyclopedia of
Men and Masculinities*, Routledge,
2007.

30 Boudet et al., 'On norms and
agency'.

31 D. Budlender, 'The statistical
evidence on care and non-care work
across six countries', Gender and
Development Programme Paper no. 4,
United Nations Research Institute for
Social Development, Geneva, 2008.

32 Barker et al., *Evolving Men*.

33 Ibid.

34 www.pewsocialtrends.
org/2013/03/14/modern-parenthood-
roles-of-moms-and-dads-converge-as-
they-balance-work-and-family/.

35 www.fira.ca/article.php?id=44.

36 www.theguardian.com/
global-development-professionals-
network/2013/nov/22/rwanda-
gender-based-violence.

37 www.guardian.co.uk/money/
2011/oct/25/stay-at-home-dads-
fathers-childcarers.

38 J. Bruce, C. Lloyd and A.
Leonard, with P. Engle and N. Duffy,
*Families in Focus: New Perspectives on
Mothers, Fathers and Children*, Popula-
tion Council, New York, 1995.

39 Stephanie Coontz, 'Why
gender equality stalled', *New York
Times*, 13 February 2013, www.ny
times.com/2013/02/17/opinion/
sunday/why-gender-equality-stalled.
html?pagewanted=all&_r=0.

40 Ibid.

41 Speaking to producer Rick
Rubin. Andrei Harmsworth, 'Jay-Z: I
could never leave a baby blue', *Metro*,
4 June 2013.

42 Interview with the author,
published in Nikki van der Gaag et al.,
'Because I am a girl: so what about
boys? State of the world's girls', Plan
International, 2011.

43 Gary Barker, *Dying to be Men:
Youth, Masculinity and Social Exclusion*,
Routledge, 2005.

44 Interview with the author.

45 Ibid.

46 Barker, *Dying to be Men*.

47 Van der Gaag et al., 'Because I
am a girl'.

48 Barker et al., *Evolving Men*.

49 V. Salles and R. Tuiran, 'Vida
familiar y democratación de los espa-
cios privados', in M. L. Fuentes and L.
Otero (eds), *La Família: Investigación y
Política Pública*, Sistema Nacional para
el Desarrollo Integral de la Familia,
Mexico City, 1996.

50 B. Garcia and O. Oliveira, 'El
ejercicio de la paternidad en México
urbano', in *Imágenes de la familia en el
cambia de siglo*, Instituto de investiga-
ciones sociales, Universidad Nacional
Autónomia de Mexico (UNAM),
Mexico City, 2004, pp. 283–317.

51 Barker et al., *Evolving Men*.

52 R. Goldman, *Fathers' Involve-
ment in their Children's Education*,
National Family and Parenting
Institute, London, 2005.

53 Barker et al., *Evolving Men*.

54 Boudet et al., 'On norms and agency'.

55 www.guardian.co.uk/lifeand style/2013/mar/23/proud-young-black-fathers.

56 Barker and Verani, 'Men's participation as fathers in the Latin American and Caribbean region'.

57 V. King, 'The antecedents and consequences of adolescents' relationships with stepfathers and nonresident fathers', *Journal of Marriage and the Family*, 68, 2006, pp. 910–28.

58 A. Sarkadi, R. Kristiansson, F. Oberklaid and S. Bremberg, 'Fathers' involvement and children's developmental outcomes: a systematic review of longitudinal studies', *Acta Pædiatrica*, 97, 2007, pp. 153–8.

59 P. Engle, T. Beardshaw and C. Loftin, 'The child's right to shared parenting', in L. Richter and R. Morell (eds), *Baba: Men and fatherhood in South Africa*, HSRC Press, Cape Town, 2006.

60 Van der Gaag et al., 'Because I am a girl'.

61 Boudet et al., 'On norms and agency'.

62 Ibid.

63 R. Crompton and C. Lyonette, 'Who does the housework? The division of labour within the home', British Social Attitudes, 24th report, National Centre for Social Research, SAGE, 2008.

64 'Men can do it! The real reasons dads don't do childcare and what men and women can do about it', ngo.media limited, 2013.

65 www.guardian.co.uk/lifeand style/2013/jul/05/childcare-men-pull-weight?INTCMP=SRCH.

66 W. Hatter et al., *Dads on Dads:*

Needs and Expectations at Home and at Work, EOC, Manchester, 2002.

67 Boudet et al., 'On norms and agency'.

68 Orly Stern, Dean Peacock and Helen Alexander (eds), *Working with Men and Boys: Emerging strategies from across Africa to address gender-based violence and HIV/AIDS*, Sonke Gender Justice Network and the MenEngage Network, 2009.

69 Barker et al., *Men Who Care*.

70 Boudet et al., 'On norms and agency'.

71 www.xyonline.net/content/hand-rocks-cradle.

72 Barker et al., *Men Who Care*.

73 www.guardian.co.uk/lifeand style/2013/jul/05/childcare-men-pull-weight?INTCMP=SRCH.

74 *Men in Families and Family Policy in a Changing World*, United Nations, New York, 2011.

75 www.mencare2.com/.

76 Interview with the author.

77 Wendy Smith and Linda Richter, 'Children's views of fathers', Fatherhood Conference, 24 November 2004

78 Richter and Morrell, *Baba: Men and Fatherhood in South Africa*.

79 T. Emmett, L. Richter, M. Makiwane, R. du Toit, H. Brookes, C. Potgieter, M. Altman and P. Makhura, *The Status of Youth Report 2003*, Umsobomvu Youth Fund, Johannesburg, 2004.

80 Richter and Morrell, *Baba: Men and Fatherhood in South Africa*.

81 Defined in Miranda Kaye and Julia Tolmie, 'Fathers' rights groups in Australia and their engagement with issues in family law', *Australian Journal of Family Law*, 12/05–01033, 1998, as: 'we have defined fathers' rights groups as being either groups which

explicitly represent fathers' concerns (whether custodial or non-custodial) or groups with an agenda which reflects the concerns of non-custodial parents (who are statistically more likely to be fathers)'.

82 www.politicalresearch.org/fathers-rights-groups-threaten-womens-gains-and-their-safety/.

83 www.now.org/nnt/03-97/father.html.

84 Rhys Price-Robertson interview with Michael Flood, 'Anti-feminist men's groups in Australia', *DVRCV Quarterly*, Spring/Summer 2012.

85 Lynne Segal, *Slow Motion: Changing Masculinities, Changing Men*, Virago, 1997.

86 Jocelyn Elise Crowley, 'Conflicted membership: women in fathers' rights groups', *Sociological Inquiry*, 79(3), August 2009, pp. 328–50.

87 www.pewsocialtrends.org/2013/03/14/modern-parenthood-roles-of-moms-and-dads-converge-as-they-balance-work-and-family/.

88 www.guardian.co.uk/lifeandstyle/2013/mar/23/proud-young-black-fathers.

89 R. Morrell, 'Of boys and men: masculinity and gender in Southern African Studies', *Journal of Southern African Studies*, 24, 1998, pp. 605–30.

90 www.youngdadstv.

91 www.men-care.org.

92 www.acev.org/english.

93 Fiona McAllister and Adrienne Burgess, in association with Jane Kato and Gary Barker, *Fatherhood: Parenting Programmes and Policy: a critical review of best practice*, Fatherhood Institute and Instituto Promundo, 2012.

94 Ibid.

95 Ibid.

96 mencarecampaign.wordpress.com/2013/04/17/bringing-in-the-love-engaging-men-as-fathers-to-end-child-marriage/.

97 Barker et al., *Evolving Men*.

98 World Health Organization, 'Fatherhood and health outcomes in Europe: a summary report', WHO Regional Office for Europe, Copenhagen, 2007.

99 www.guardian.co.uk/lifeandstyle/2013/jul/05/childcare-men-pull-weight?INTCMP=SRCH.

7 Proving their manhood

1 Orly Stern, Dean Peacock and Helen Alexander (eds), *Working with Men and Boys: Emerging strategies from across Africa to address gender-based violence and HIV/AIDS*, Sonke Gender Justice Network and the MenEngage Network 2009.

2 newint.org/features/2011/07/01/boys-brazils-favelas-violence-against-women/.

3 Not his real name.

4 Interview with the author.

5 Nishtha Chugh, 'A drive to beat Rwanda's gender-based violence', *Guardian*, 22 November 2013, www.theguardian.com/global-development-professionals-network/2013/nov/22/rwanda-gender-based-violence.

6 www.guardian.co.uk/lifeandstyle/the-womens-blog-with-janemartinson/2013/apr/30/saudi-arabia-domestic-violence-campaign.

7 www.awid.org/Media/Files/WITM_Preliminary_2011_results.

8 www.unifem.org/gender_issues/violence_against_women/.

9 WHO, 'Global and regional estimates of violence against women: prevalence and health effects of intimate partner violence and non-partner sexual violence', Department of Reproductive Health and Research,

London School of Hygiene and Tropical Medicine, South African Medical Research Council, 2013.

10 www.mtlsa.org/2012/10/3-women-die-day-due-domestic-violence/.

11 'The nature, extent, incidence and impact of domestic violence against women in the states of Andhra Pradesh, Chhattisgarh, Gujarat, Madhya Pradesh and Maharashtra', submitted to the Planning Commission, Government of India, New Delhi.

12 'Violence against women: an EU-wide survey: main results', European Union Agency for Fundamental rights, 2014.

13 '"Keeping silence is dying": results from the national study on domestic violence against women in Viet Nam', General Statistics Office, Hanoi.

14 www.theguardian.com/uk-news/2013/sep/03/caroline-criado-perez-rape-threats-continue.

15 www.everydaysexism.com/.

16 www.theguardian.com/lifeand style/the-womens-blog-with-jane-martinson/2013/apr/16/everyday-sexism-project-shouting-back.

17 http://www.mybangalore. com/article/0810/its-not-common-anymore-an-online-campaign-against-eve-teasing.html.

18 WHO, *World Report on Violence and Health*, World Health Organization, Geneva, 2002.

19 Ibid.

20 *Multiple Indicator Cluster Survey Vietnam 2011: Key Findings*, General Statistics Office, Hanoi, 2012.

21 World Health Organization and London School of Hygiene and Tropical Medicine, *Preventing Intimate Partner and Sexual Violence against Women*, World Health Organization, Geneva, 2010.

22 S. Burton et al., 'Young people's attitudes towards violence, sex and relationships, Scotland: zero tolerance trust', 1998, quoted in J. Mirsky, *Beyond Victims and Villains*, Panos, 2004.

23 Rachel Jewkes, Yandisa Sikweyiya, Robert Morrell and Kristin Dunkle, 'Understanding men's health and use of violence: interface of rape and HIV in South Africa', MRC Policy Brief, 2009, www.mrc.ac.za/gender/ violence_hiv.pdf.

24 www.comacare.com.

25 Chugh, 'A drive to beat Rwanda's gender-based violence: case studies', www.theguardian.com/ global-development-professionals-network/2013/nov/22/rwanda-gender-based-violence-case-studies.

26 Interview with the author.

27 WHO, *World Report on Violence and Health*.

28 www.mencanstoprape.org/poll 3535/poll_show.htm?doc_id=220239.

29 National Center for PTSD, 2007.

30 www.bbc.co.uk/news/uk-13661407.

31 J. C. Babcock, S. A. Miller and C. Siard, 'Toward a typology of abusive women: differences between partner-only and generally violent women in the use of violence', *Psychology of Women Quarterly*, 27, 2003, pp. 153–61.

32 S. C. Swan and D. L. Snow, 'Behavioral and psychological differences among abused women who use violence in intimate relationships', *Violence Against Women*, 9, 2003, pp. 75–109.

33 G. L. Stuart, T. M. Moore, K. C. Gordon, J. C. Hellmuth, S. E. Ramsey and C. W. Kahler, 'Reasons for intimate partner violence perpetra-

tion among arrested women', *Violence Against Women*, 12, 2006, pp. 609–21.

34 Nikki van der Gaag et al., 'Because I am a girl: so what about boys? State of the world's girls', Plan International, 2011.

35 www.ipsnews.net/2013/04/austerity-leaves-domestic-violence-victims-stranded/.

36 'Violence against women: an EU-wide survey: main results'.

37 Michael Kaufman, 'The seven P's of men's violence', in Michael S. Kimmel and Michael A. Messner, *Men's Lives*, 9th edn, Pearson, 2013.

38 newint.org/features/2011/07/01/boys-brazils-favelas-violence-against-women/.

39 http://www.thoughtleader.co.za/melaniejudge/2013/04/03/behind-the-shock-and-awe-the-violence-is-normal/.

40 www.ipsnews.net/2013/04/austerity-leaves-domestic-violence-victims-stranded/.

41 L. Heise, 'Violence against women: an integrated, ecological framework', *Violence Against Women*, 4, 1998, pp. 262–90.

42 Chugh, 'A drive to beat Rwanda's gender-based violence: case studies'.

43 Western Balkan Gender-based Violence Prevention Initiative, *Exploring Dimensions of Masculinity and Violence*, CARE and ICRW, 2007.

44 Interview with the author.

45 Kristin L. Dunkle, Rachel Jewkes, Mzikazi Nduna, Nwabisa Jama, Jonathon Levin, Yandisa Sikweyiya and Mary P Koss, 'Transactional sex with casual and main partners among young South African men in the rural Eastern Cape: prevalence, predictors, and associations with gender-based violence', *Social Science & Medicine*,

65(6), September 2007; Will H. Courtenay, 'Constructions of masculinity and their influence on men's well-being: a theory of gender and health', *Social Science & Medicine*, 50(10), May, 2000; James R. Mahalik, S. Burns and Matthew Syzdek, 'Masculinity and perceived normative health behaviors as predictors of men's health behaviors', *Social Science & Medicine*, 64(11), March 2007.

46 Gary Barker, Manuel Contreras, Brian Heilman, Ajay Singh, Ravi Verma and Marcos Nascimento, 'Evolving men: initial results from the international men and gender equality survey', International Center for Research on Women and Instituto Promundo, 2011.

47 Western Balkan Gender-based Violence Prevention Initiative, *Exploring Dimensions of Masculinity and Violence*.

48 WHO, *World Report on Violence and Health*.

49 bell hooks, *The Will to Change: Men, masculinities and love*, Washington Square Press, New York, 2003.

50 Western Balkan Gender-based Violence Prevention Initiative, *Exploring Dimensions of Masculinity and Violence*.

51 Barker et al., 'Evolving men'.

52 '"I'd rather be hit with a stick … grades are sacred": students' perceptions of discipline and authority in a public high school in Peru', Working Paper 70, Young Lives, 2011.

53 Lori Heise, 'What works to prevent partner violence: an evidence overview', STRIVE Research Consortium, London, 2011.

54 Barker et al., 'Evolving men'.

55 UNICEF, *State of the World's Children*, 2007.

56 G. Barker and C. Ricardo, 'Young men and the construction of

masculinity in sub-Saharan Africa: implications for HIV/AIDS, conflict, and violence', Social Development Papers no. 26, World Bank, Washington, DC, June 2005.

57 Heise, 'What works to prevent partner violence'.

58 Western Balkan Gender-based Violence Prevention Initiative, *Exploring Dimensions of Masculinity and Violence*.

59 Gary Barker, *Dying to be Men: Youth, masculinity and social exclusion*, Routledge, London, 2005.

60 Barker et al., *Evolving Men*.

61 Barker, Gary, Manuel Contreras, Brian Heilman, Ajay Singh, Ravi Verma, and Marcos Nascimento. 'Evolving men: Initial results from the international men and gender equality survey.' International Center for Research on Women and Instituto Promundo, 2011.

62 Tu-Anh Hoang, Tang Thu Quach and Tam Thanh Tran, 'Because I am a man, I should be gentle to my wife and children: positive masculinity to stop gender-based violence in a coastal district of Vietnam', *Gender and Development*, 21(1): 81–96.

63 Ian Bannon and Maria C. Correia, 'The other half of gender: men's issues in development', World Bank, 2006.

64 Duncan Green, Richard King and May Miller-Dawkins, 'The global economic crisis and developing countries', Oxfam International Research Report, May 2010.

65 WHO, *World Report on Violence and Health*.

66 Heise, 'What works to prevent partner violence'.

67 silentnomore.org/after-the-assault/information-for-men/male-victims/.

68 www.guardian.co.uk/global-development-professionals-network/2013/jun/25/dealing-with-male-rape.

69 'Promoting accountability for conflict-related sexual violence against men: a comparative legal analysis of international and domestic laws relating to IDP and refugee men in Uganda', Refugee Law Project Working Paper no. 24, July 2013.

70 Ibid.

71 Inger Agger, 'Sexual torture of political prisoners: an overview', *J.Traumatic Stress*, 2(3), 1989, pp. 311–12.

72 Željka Mudrovčić, 'Sexual and gender-based violence in post-conflict regions: the Bosnia and Herzegovina case', in 'The impact of armed conflict on women and girls: a consultative meeting on mainstreaming gender in areas of conflict and reconstruction', United Nations Population Fund, 2011.

73 Anthony R. Jones and George R. Fay, 'AR 15-6 Investigation of the Abu Ghraib detention facility and 205th Military Intelligence Brigade 68-69', 2005, www.globalsecurity.org/intell/library/reports/2004/intell-abu-ghraib_ar15-6.pdf.

74 See www.saartjiebaartmancentre.org.za/.

75 Interview with the author.

76 Barker et al., *Evolving Men*.

77 www.guardian.co.uk/commentisfree/2011/mar/12/celtic-rangers-glasgow-domestic-violence.

78 www.thoughtleader.co.za/melaniejudge/2013/04/03/behind-the-shock-and-awe-the-violence-is-normal/.

79 Alexia Cooper and Erica Smith, *Homicide Trends in the United States, 1980–2008*, Bureau of Justice Statistics, 2011, www.bjs.gov/index.cfm?ty=pbdetail&iid=2221.

80 Barker, *Dying to be Men*.

81 Instituto Brasiliero de Geo-grafia e Estatistica (IBGE), 2004, quoted in Barker, *Dying to be Men*.

82 www.huffingtonpost.com/gary-barker-phd/brazils-undeclared-war-on_b_4647204.html.

83 Barker et al., *Evolving Men*.

84 www.policymic.com/articles/40049/nra-vendor-sells-ex-girlfriend-target-that-bleeds-when-you-shoot-it.

85 Van der Gaag et al., 'Because I am a girl'.

86 Amnesty UK, *Sexual Assault Research*, Amnesty, London, 2005.

87 Jose Reyes Mori and Angel Palacios Trujillo, 'Una experiencia de trabajo con varones que ejercen violencia familiar en el distrito de San Juan de Lurigancho: construy-endo masculinidades sin violencia, camiando maneras de pensar, sentir y actuar', Centre Mujet Teresa de Jesus, Lima, 2010 (quoted in *Gender and Development*).

88 Van der Gaag et al., 'Because I am a girl', *The State of the World's Girls 2008* Special Focus: 'In the Shadow of War', Plan International.

89 Barker et al., *Evolving Men*.

90 Alan Greig, Dean Peacock, Rachel Jewkes and Sisonke Msimang, 'Gender and AIDS: time to act', *AIDS 2008*, 22(suppl. 2): S35–S43. Copyright © Lippincott Williams & Wilkins.

91 edition.cnn.com/2013/07/22/world/meast/uae-norway-rape-controversy/index.html?hpt=hp_c2.

92 newint.org/blog/2013/01/03/delhi-gang-rape-death/.

93 onebillionrising.org/.

94 www.whiteribbon.com

95 www.mencanstoprape.org/info-url2696/info-url_list.htm?section=Men%20of%20Strength%20%28MOST%29%20Clubs.

96 mavaw.org/.

97 Tu-Anh Hoang et al., 'Because I am a man, I should be gentle to my wife and children'.

98 www.youtube.com/watch?v=u4FupHdNghg.

99 Interview with the author.

100 men-care.org/Programs/MenCare002B.aspx.

101 www.genderjustice.org.za/onemancan/home/index.php.

102 www.thejakartapost.com/news/2013/12/15/healthy-happy-wives-begin-with-caring-men.html.

103 www.bellbajao.org/.

104 www.bellbajao.org/home/about/.

105 www.everydaysexism.com.

106 www.theguardian.com/lifeandstyle/womens-blog/2014/mar/14/men-fight-against-everyday-sexism-gender-inequality.

107 Ibid.

8 Conclusion

1 See, for example, www.theguardian.com/commentisfree/2013/dec/09/black-feminist-movement-fails-women-black-minority.

2 www.channel4.com/news/twitter-troll-guilty-feminist-caroline-criado-perez.

3 time.com/14543/calling-all-men-gender-equality-isnt-just-a-female-cause/.

4 Interview with the author.

5 Kat Banyard, *The Equality Illusion: The truth about men and women today*, Faber and Faber, London, 2010.

SELECTED READING

Banyard, Kat (2010) *The Equality Illusion: The truth about men and women today*, London: Faber and Faber.

Barker, Gary (2005) *Dying to be Men: Youth, masculinities and social exclusion*, London: Routledge.

Barker, G., J. M. Contreras, B. Heilman, A. K. Singh, R. K. Verma and M. Nascimento (2011) *Evolving Men: Initial Results from the International Men and Gender Equality Survey* (IMAGES), Washington, DC/Rio de Janeiro: International Center for Research on Women/Instituto Promundo.

Barker, Gary, in collaboration with Margaret Greene and Marcos Nascimento (2012) *Men Who Care: A Multi-Country Qualitative Study of Men in Non-Traditional Caregiving Roles*, Men and Gender Equality Policy Project (MGEPP), led by Instituto Promundo and the International Center for Research on Women (ICRW).

Cleaver, Francis (2002) *Masculinities Matter! Men, gender and development*, London: Zed Books.

Connell, R. W. (2002) *Gender*, Cambridge: Polity Press.

— (2005) 'Change among the gatekeepers: men, masculinities, and gender equality in the global arena', *Signs*, 30: 1801–25.

Cornwall, Andrea, Jerker Edström and Alan Grieg (eds) (2011) *Men and Development: Politicizing masculinities*, London: Zed Books.

Digby, Tom (ed.) (1998) *Men Doing Feminism*, London: Routledge.

Eliot, Lise (2010) *Pink Brain, Blue Brain: How Small Differences Grow into Troublesome Gaps – and What We Can Do about It*, New York: Mariner Books.

Faludi, Susan (1999) *Stiffed: The Betrayal of the Modern Man*, London: Chatto and Windus.

Fine, Cordelia (2010) *Delusions of Gender: The Real Science behind Sex Differences*, London: Icon Books.

Flood, Michael, Judith Kegan Gardiner, Bob Pease and Keith Pringle (eds) (2007) *International Encyclopedia of Men and Masculinities*, London: Routledge.

Fraser, Nancy (2013) *Fortunes of Feminism: From State-managed Capitalism to Neoliberal Crisis*, London: Verso.

Gender & Development (2013) 'Working with men on gender equality', 21(1), March, Oxfam.

Goldrick-Jones, Amanda (2002) *Men Who Believe in Feminism*, New York: Praeger.

Hawkes, A. and K. Buse (2013) 'Gender and global health: evidence, policy, and inconvenient truths', *The Lancet*, 381: 1783–7.

hooks, bell (2000) *Feminism Is for Everybody: Passionate politics*, London: Pluto Press.

— (2003) *The Will to Change: Men, masculinities and love*, New York: Washington Square Press.

Johnson, Allan G. (2005) *The Gender*

Knot: Unravelling our patriarchal legacy, Philadelphia, PA: Temple University Press.

Katz, Jackson (2006) *The Macho Paradox, Why Some Men Hurt Women and How All Men Can Help*, Illinois: Sourcebooks.

Kaufman, Michael and Michael Kimmel (2011) *The Guy's Guide to Feminism*, Berkeley, CA: Seal Press.

Kimmel, Michael (2008) *Guyland: The Perilous World Where Guys Become Men*, Lonson: HarperCollins.

Kimmel, Michael S. and Thomas E. Mosmiller (1992) *Against the Tide: Pro-Feminist Men in the United States: 1776–1990, a Documentary History*, Boston, MA: Beacon Press.

McAllister, Fiona and Adrienne Burgess, in association with Jane Kato and Gary Barker (2012) *Fatherhood: Parenting Programmes and Policy: A Critical review of best practice*, Fatherhood Institute and Instituto Promundo.

Moran, Caitlin (2012) *How to Be a Woman*, London: HarperCollins.

Munoz Boudet, Ana Maria, Patti Petesch and Carolyn Turk, with Angelica Thumala (2012) *On Norms and Agency: Conversations about Gender Equality with Women and Men in 20 Countries*, World Bank.

Redfern, Catherine and Kristin Aune (2010) *Reclaiming the F Word*, London: Zed Books.

Richter, Linda and Robert Morrell (eds) (2006) *Baba: Men and fatherhood in South Africa*, Cape Town: HSRC Press.

Roisin, Hanna (2012) *The End of Men and the Rise of Women*, London: Penguin/Viking.

Ruxton, Sandy (ed.) (2004) *Gender Equality and Men: Learning from Practice*, Oxfam GB.

Sandberg, Sheryl (2013) *Lean In: Women, work and the will to lead*, New York: Random House.

Segal, Lynne (1990) *Slow Motion: Changing Masculinities, Changing Men*, London: Virago.

Stern, Orly, Dean Peacock and Helen Alexander (2009) *Working with Men and Boys: Emerging strategies from across Africa to address gender-based violence and HIV/AIDS*, Sonke Gender Justice Network and the MenEngage Network.

Tarrant, Shira (2009) *Men and Feminism*, Berkeley, CA: Seal Press.

Valenti, Jessica (2007) *Full Frontal Feminism: A young woman's guide to why feminism matters*, Berkeley, CA: Seal Press.

Van der Gaag, Nikki (2008) *The No-Nonsense Guide to Women's Rights*, New Internationalist.

Van der Gaag, Nikki et al. (2011) 'Because I am a girl: so what about boys? State of the world's girls', Plan International.

Way, Niobe (2011) *Deep Secrets: Boys' friendships and the crisis of connection*, Cambridge, MA: Harvard University Press.

Selected websites on men and gender equality

www.genderjustice.org.za/
www.promundo.org.br/en/
www.men-care-org
www.menengage.org
www.whiteribbon.com
site.nomas.org/
www.xyonline.net/

INDEX